Child and Adolescent Migration, Mental Health, and Language

LANGUAGE, DISCOURSE AND MENTAL HEALTH

Series Editors:

**Laura A. Cariola, Lecturer in Applied Psychology
at the University of Edinburgh**

**Billy Lee, Lecturer in Psychology at the
University of Edinburgh**

**Lisa Mikesell, Associate Professor of Communication
at Rutgers University, USA**

**Michael Birch, Professor of English & Communications
at Massachusetts College of Liberal Arts, USA**

Mental Health Ontologies
How We Talk About Mental Health, and Why it Matters in the Digital Age
Janna Hastings, 2020

Madness and Literature
What Fiction Can Do for the Understanding of Mental Illness
ed. Lasse R. Gammelgaard, 2022

Eating Disorders in Public Discourse
Exploring Media Representations and Lived Experiences
ed. Laura A. Cariola, 2023

Child and Adolescent Migration, Mental Health, and Language
Effects of Trauma and Foreign Language Immersions
Fernanda Carra-Salsberg

CHILD AND ADOLESCENT MIGRATION, MENTAL HEALTH, AND LANGUAGE

Effects of Trauma and Foreign Language Immersions

Fernanda Carra-Salsberg

UNIVERSITY
of
EXETER
PRESS

First published in 2024 by
University of Exeter Press
Reed Hall, Streatham Drive
Exeter EX4 4QR, UK

www.exeterpress.co.uk

Child and Adolescent Migration, Mental Health, and Language: Effects of Trauma and Foreign Language Immersions

Copyright © 2024 Fernanda Carra-Salsberg

The right of Fernanda Carra-Salsberg to be identified as author of this work has been asserted by her in accordance with the Copyright, Designs and Patents Act 1988.

Language, Discourse and Mental Health

ISSN 3049-7205 Print
ISSN 3049-7213 Online

https://doi.org/10.47788/NLCS3918

British Library Cataloguing in Publication Data
A catalogue record for this book is available from the British Library.

ISBN 978-1-80413-039-1 Hbk
ISBN 978-1-80413-040-7 ePub
ISBN 978-1-80413-041-4 PDF

Cover image: iStock.com//photominus

Typeset in Caslon and Myriad by S4Carlisle Publishing Services, Chennai, India

In loving memory of my cousin Max
(1996–2021)

Contents

Acknowledgements	viii
Introduction—Transnational Migrations: Addressing New Concerns for an Old Practice	1
1 Dialogic Encounters: Conceptualizing Effects on Belief Systems, Subjectivities, and Individuals' Personal and Shared Histories	9
2 Migration and Trauma: Defining the Problem of Child and Adolescent Transnational Relocations	26
3 Memory within Language: Our Mother Tongue's Link to Subjective Development and our Remembered and Seemingly Forgotten Sense of Being, Loving, and Belonging	44
4 Trauma's Dimension within and outside Language	69
5 Bearing Witness to Translingual Realities: A Study of the Significance of First-Person, Cross-Cultural Publications	91
6 How to Conclude from Here?	117
Notes	130
References	139
Index	148

Acknowledgements

I would like to begin by expressing my sincere gratitude to Laura Cariola, Hetty Marx, Anna Henderson, and Nigel Massen from University of Exeter Press. Thank you for the trust that has been bestowed upon me for the completion of this project. Thank you to Dr Joseph Fernando from the Toronto Psychoanalytic Institute for reading parts of my manuscript and sharing your work and insights on trauma. Thanks to Dr Kaspars Tuters, also from the Toronto Psychoanalytic Institute, for sharing your research and experience working with child and adolescent migrants.

A heartfelt thanks to my devoted husband, Paul Salsberg, and to our loving daughters, Abi and Madi. I am extremely grateful for your patience and support during my seemingly endless hours working on this book. To my parents, Basilio and Marta Carra, thank you for imagining a future in a new country, with a foreign language and a culture that differed greatly from our own. A warm thank you to my extended family and my close friends in Canada, for helping me build a strong sense of home away from my original home. A special thank you to our family in Argentina, for staying in touch and loving us despite our distance.

At last, and in light of the most recent acts of terrorism affecting the Middle East, I would also like to dedicate this publication to its many victims. May there be an end to the dehumanization of minors and adults and to the never-ending, worldwide propagation of hate. May this generation and later generations understand the insurmountable injustice and traumas inflicted on civilians on both sides of the conflict. May we learn from mistakes, find a sustainable solution, and aid in the individual and shared recovery from this horrifying tragedy.

Introduction

Transnational Migrations: Addressing New Concerns for an Old Practice

As of 2017, the United Nations counts 68.5 million people who were forcibly displaced worldwide, 24.5 million of which are considered refugees. The numbers are so staggering that you forget these are people forced to leave their homes. They are doctors and teachers. Lawyers, journalists, poets, and priests. And children, so many children ... refugees are ordinary people. All that differentiates them is that they got caught in the middle of a conflict that forced them to leave their homes ... it is too often a choice between life and death ... [and] as my family did a decade ago, they chose life.

(Yousafzai 2019: x–xi)

There is no newness to migration. Individuals, families, and entire communities have been on the move since time immemorial. For several known and unknown reasons, even before territories became delineated by the politics and laws that currently govern them, crossing regions, landforms, as well as cultural and linguistic borders has been a common occurrence in many, if not all, civilizations. In today's era of increasing transnational movements, the reasons behind international relocations are commonly known. We do not need to be experts on present-day refugee crises or fervid media followers to grasp, at least in part, the realities behind the images and stories disseminated online, on podcasts, on our television screens, and in newspapers across the globe. We know that the extraordinary numbers of present-day border crossings result from the escalation of unmet human needs. Often international relocations

CHILD AND ADOLESCENT MIGRATION, MENTAL HEALTH, AND LANGUAGE

take place when individuals and entire families are deprived of viable opportunities for an optimal or sustainable present and future.

While temporary workers and economic migrants cross borders in search of work, and international students travel to gain novel experiences or a better education, an escalating number of individuals, young and old, able-bodied and disabled, are on the move to escape unsafe conditions. Reasons for their migrations include yet are not limited to the need to access food, drinking water, shelter, and/or reliable healthcare. People traverse international borders after becoming displaced by natural disasters that often result from the detrimental effects of global warming. Some relocate in a search for social justice, and/or opportunities for equal education. Others try escaping the devastating consequences of armed conflicts, generalized and organized violence, human rights violations, and fears of persecution.[1]

Trauma and post-traumatic stress disorder (PTSD) are common psychological conditions among those who have been displaced (McGregor, Melvin & Newman 2015: 371). Individuals and entire families migrate to escape their hometowns after being subjected to life-changing occurrences. Many individuals witness death, torture, wars, sexual abuse, and disappearance and/or wrongful imprisonment of loved ones and/or neighbours. Yet, regardless of the dire circumstances they experience, many asylum seekers encounter significant barriers when trying to relocate through legal channels. Hence, out of desperation and a lack of viable options, many individuals and families take part in high-priced, illegal, and unsafe border crossings.

For young migrants, the stress and anxiety involved in both licit and illicit border crossings increase when they travel without the care and protection of well-intended adults. Nonetheless, not all minors migrate as part of family units. Some children and adolescents travel unaccompanied after being separated from their parents and/or loved ones during incidences of violence (Ensor 2016: 62) and/or natural disasters. Too often, however, forced and chosen separations are by-products of countries' strict reception systems. As addressed in this book's first chapter, separations may be imposed when families arrive undocumented at border crossings. Chosen separations, on the other hand, may occur prior to minors' attempt to cross—specifically, when adults deduce that travelling as a family unit would decrease the likelihood of their children reaching the desired country.

As highlighted by Sutterlüty and Tisdall (2019), not all unaccompanied children are orphaned, or forcefully separated from their families. Many

2

INTRODUCTION

minors are willing individuals with agency who are supported by their parents or loved ones. In such cases, adults pay smugglers to have their willing children and adolescents cross international borders. Minors' involvement in this illicit journey is founded in their desperation and strong need to escape extreme conditions that threaten their lives and well-being. Unfortunately, aside from risking their lives when engaging in illegal crossings, too often unprotected minors become unwilling victims or willing agents of sexual exploitation (183).

Whether minors are documented or undocumented, whether they are migrants, refugees, or asylum seekers, and whether they arrive alone or as part of family units, their known and unknown, imaginable and unimaginable struggles do not end when they arrive at destination countries. In resettlement countries, disorienting uncertainties often add to newcomers' vulnerability, powerlessness, cumulative stressors, and trauma(s). The sudden change of newcomers' subject position combined with the symbolic, systemic, and sometimes physical violence that conditions their experiences also become concerning factors that affect migrants' sense of physical safety and psycho-emotional well-being.

In transit and destination countries, the uncertainty of newcomers' future affects their ability to adapt and thrive in their new environment. Financial struggles and substandard housing conditions only add to their vulnerable condition. Stigmatization and discrimination, especially of racialized individuals, place adults and adolescents at a greater risk of harassment and abuse. While it is not uncommon for newcomers to work long, irregular hours, many migrants find themselves under- or unemployed. Undocumented workers, young and old, are often subjected to poor working conditions, violence, and exploitation. For many migrants, their financial struggles often lead to housing and food insecurity, limited access to medicine, poorly met medical assistance, and restricted access to social services.

With a focus on child and adolescent migrants, we understand that education is a human right that is meant to aid in students' cognitive and social development, their life outcomes, and their overall well-being. In agreement with Douglas et al. (2020), 'schools not only provide an education, but are a haven, a source of food, an opportunity to identify abuse, and an important platform to receive information' (n.p.). Yet, as seen in countries like Canada, for minors to enrol in public schools, they require proof of legal residence. While exceptions are sometimes unofficially made by school administrators, without proper

3

documentation and out of fear of deportation, many undocumented minors are forced to forgo an education. By extension, these children and adolescents are denied access to a system and to programmes that are meant to educate, identify potential problems in minors' homes, guide caregivers, and help students with possible academic, social, and mental health concerns.

Make Up of the Book

Child and Adolescent Migration, Mental Health, and Language: Effects of Trauma and Foreign Language Immersions takes an expanded approach to the problem of international relocations. This study is grounded in psychoanalytic, semiotic, language socialization, trauma, and critical race theories. It looks at the personal, pedagogic, and political significance of cross-cultural publications. Specifically, it studies the importance of analysing published testimonies of adults looking back at their reconstructed memories of being young migrants.

Originally, this project was solely centred on the affective significance of a first language. It was meant to focus on language's influence on minors' foreign-host sociolinguistic immersions and host-/second-language acquisition. This publication was also to examine language's link to migrants' conscious and unconscious traumas, and the significance of testimonial auto-narratives. Yet as research continued and notes grew in length, it became clear that the preliminary observations only partially illustrated a much larger, highly complex picture. Not looking at conditions that lead to relocations, and not accounting for the politics that shape pre- and post-migration experiences, limited readers' understanding of young migrants' short- and long-term challenges.

While never denying the helpful efforts carried out by governments and organizations across the world, or the potential long-term positive impact of migration, this volume critically examines the complexity of international relocations. It focuses on the challenges and traumas children and adolescents encounter prior to, during, and following their journeys. It draws attention to common receiving systems, and how these add to the barriers to safe migration and newcomers' positive adjustment and well-being.

Without departing from its main focus, this volume also considers how an internalized language grounds us socially, geographically, culturally, and historically. It draws attention to the ways in which this private yet shared

INTRODUCTION

phenomenon influences individuals' ongoing conceptualizations, belief systems, behaviours, as well as speakers' sense of belonging and unbelonging within their surrounding environments. It contends that studying a lived, primary language's inner and social significance grants us a glimpse of newcomers' initial disorientation. Such focus sheds light on the inner and social crises that many experienced during their initial period of subjective location, dislocation, and relocation. Equally importantly, this study suggests that sharing the overwhelming nature of past and present vicissitudes within, between, and outside language(s) may lead to a synthesis of poorly understood cumulative trauma(s) from the writer, and to a—much needed—empathy from readers.

The book is divided into the following six chapters.

CHAPTER 1—Dialogic Encounters: Conceptualizing Effects on Belief Systems, Subjectivities, and Individuals' Personal and Shared Histories

With a focus on dominant belief systems, Chapter 1 draws attention to the manner in which dialogic processes may affect migrants' experiences before, during, and following their geographic, sociocultural, and linguistic relocations. While not disregarding the benefits that stem from international migrations, this chapter offers a look into the contemporary concerns influencing young migrants' socio-affective experiences within the intricate political condition of migrancy.[2] This is accomplished through the examination of individuals' known and unknown involvement in the dispersion of belief systems that stigmatize and other. This chapter examines the complex relationship between immigration, racialization, and racism. It also draws the link between countries' nationalist sentiments, immigration policies, and receiving practices. Its purpose is to lay the foundation for a better understanding of this book's following three chapters, which are centred on the accumulation of challenges newcomers often encounter in home, transit, and receiving countries. Such focus is intended to aid in our understanding of how the amalgamation of young migrants' crises has an inevitable short- and long-term effect on their subjective development and mental health. By looking closely at the sociopolitical significance of language, this chapter makes way for the study of language's subjective meaning and its involvement in individuals' development and adaptation following their international relocations.

CHILD AND ADOLESCENT MIGRATION, MENTAL HEALTH, AND LANGUAGE

CHAPTER 2—Migration and Trauma: Defining the Problem of Child and Adolescent Transnational Relocations

With a continued focus on international movements, Chapter 2 examines the challenges migrants, refugees, and asylum seekers often encounter prior to, during, and following their migration. It outlines the differing types of relocations and their link to migrants' status within receiving countries. It also highlights how such status influences children's potential access to resources and services. This chapter draws attention to family separation and the conditions affecting minors at hotspots, makeshift and government-run camps, and detention centres. It studies the challenges families and unaccompanied minors experience while being on the move, and also explores the international laws that are in place to protect the rights of minors. It examines how, with irregular entries in countries like Canada, minors' rights and well-being are not always at the forefront of immediate attention.

CHAPTER 3—Memory within Language: Our Mother Tongue's Link to our Subjective Development and our Remembered and Seemingly Forgotten Sense of Being, Loving, and Belonging

Following a discussion of the link of language with individuals' conscious, preconscious, and unconscious realities, Chapter 3 takes a psychoanalytic approach to the study of how our emotions, thoughts, attitudes, and behaviours are influenced by an admixture of internal and external forces. It looks at how such factors relate to perceived and seemingly forgotten histories. Through the analysis of memoirs written by former child and adolescent migrants, this chapter highlights how our primary language—or mother tongue—is unconsciously linked to our first objects of affection, ego development, first individuation, attachments, and introjections of dominant belief systems. Adding to Chapter 1's semiotic approach, this chapter studies what is at the core of individuals' large-group identities. Specifically, it examines how introjections and attachments affect the manner in which migrants become marginalized and stigmatized in transit and destination countries. This chapter also takes a psychoanalytic approach to second-language learning. It argues that a primary language, whether spoken or perceptually ignored, is associated with our earliest maternal imago, and thus etched in our unconscious memories in the form of unarticulated feelings. Conceptualizing our language's significance within our history of affect is essential to understanding migrants' emotional relation with their mother tongue. Grasping our language's emotional currency is also key to understanding young migrants' short- and long-term responses to the introjection of a new language and its foreign reality.

CHAPTER 4—Trauma's Dimension within and outside Language

With a continued focus on international migrations, Chapter 4 examines the relationship between migration, language, and trauma. It offers theories on trauma as well as psychoanalytic discussions centred on the developmental stages of childhood and adolescence. This chapter explores the difficulties most young newcomers encounter when going through life's transitions as migrants. It also pays close attention to how negative, extraordinary occurrences inflict upon minors' psycho-emotional development. After highlighting the developmental importance of primary caregivers in children's and adolescents' lives, this section turns readers' attention to the challenges minors may encounter when trying to navigate through their cumulative crises without their caregivers' physical and/or emotional presence and support.

CHAPTER 5—Bearing Witness to Translingual Realities: A Study of the Significance of First-Person, Cross-Cultural Publications

Individuals exposed to trauma commonly share the need to articulate the experiences that led to their past and/or present distress. Accordingly, extending our discussion of the ways in which young migrants' internalized languages bear witness to a conscious and unconscious set of cumulative crises, this chapter focuses on the importance of writers engaging in the creative process of remembering, imagining, reconceptualizing, synthesizing, and therefore healing through language. By studying auto-narratives written by former child and adolescent migrants, this chapter examines the significance of adults' memories in the construction and understanding of their childhood and adolescent experiences and traumas. In addition to exploring the therapeutic and developmental significance of learning from sharing one's own experiences, this section is also relevant to pedagogy and curriculum writing. It highlights the significance of teaching English through reflections, testimony, and the understanding of writers' experiences within the realm of migrancy, otherness, language learning, and developmental growth.

CHAPTER 6—How to Conclude from Here?

This book turns readers' attention to the traumas that result from push factors, relocations, international policies, and receiving systems. It highlights how in today's era of ever-increasing international migrations, children's and adolescents' realities become a part of an overwhelming accumulation of crises and resulting traumas. As argued throughout this volume, the overwhelming nature and cumulative effects of migration give way to individuals' ensuing need to share, triangulate, understand, and eventually heal. The challenges defined by the needs, uncertainties, and politics that engulf migrants' lives before, during, and following their relocations are intertwined with the disorientation that stems from becoming suddenly immersed within a compound foreign reality.

This final chapter points to the need for international awareness: a genuine understanding of the complex realities affecting young migrants and, when applicable, their families. It highlights the pressing need for systemic changes at the psychological, medical, and educational levels. With a focus on newcomers' individual and shared sociopolitical and subjective experiences, this study also asks psychologists, psychiatrists, healthcare professionals, and pedagogues working with young migrants to develop sensitive and sensible, culturally responsive approaches to helping minors as they struggle with the complexity of their experiences. At the socio-psychological and academic levels, this volume points to the need to guide both children and caregivers as they navigate their way through the turbulent ever-changing linguistic, social, and affective challenges of migrancy.

1 Dialogic Encounters: Conceptualizing Effects on Belief Systems, Subjectivities, and Individuals' Personal and Shared Histories

> The world is not humane just because it is made of human beings, and it does not become humane just because the human voice sounds in it, but only when it has become the object of discourse ... We humanize what is going on in the world and in ourselves only by speaking of it, and in the course of speaking of it we learn to be human.
>
> Arendt 1993: 24

Following the horrors of the Holocaust, Hannah Arendt spent many years conceptualizing the private and shared realities that influence individuals' behaviours and sociopolitical worlds. With a focus on history, this German-born Jewish thinker looked at our ability to adapt and transform. She described the limitations of all existence—natality and mortality—as well as our potential for freedom through action—work and labour. According to Arendt, our freedom relies on our capacity to reason and share common concerns and individual points of view. It is also founded on our ability to 'start something' by thinking outside dominant dialectical frameworks (Baehr 2000: 20–21). To be human, argues Arendt, is not inherent, nor is it ever 'acquired in solitude'.[1] Instead, it is learned through a network of relations, by means of interactions— our willingness and ability to listen, understand, and think in place of the Other. While primarily influenced by philosophers such as Plato and Immanuel Kant, and later by Karl Jaspers and Martin Heidegger, Arendt sees thinking and resulting behaviours as the basis of our humanness. Hence, fulfilling our potential concerns, having a voice, conceptualizing, and rationally pursuing

CHILD AND ADOLESCENT MIGRATION, MENTAL HEALTH, AND LANGUAGE

our goals are values highlighted in much of her work. Learning to be human, she claims, also involves taking responsibility and transforming our worlds (xxviii). In other words, it entails becoming agents, however possible, within the complexity of our experiences.

Even though Arendt's discussions have mainly focused on political theory, I have always been drawn to the manner in which her arguments pay close attention to the socio-cognitive and subjective significance of language. In her book *The Human Condition*, Arendt (1998) argues that our 'evolution of human, out of animal life' is primarily made possible through speech:[2]

> Words and deeds reveal who we are ... Many, and even most acts are performed in the manner of speech. Without the accompaniment of speech ... action ... would lose its subject ... [a] deed ... becomes relevant only through the spoken word in which he [man] identifies himself as the actor, announcing what he does, has done, and intends to do.
>
> In acting and speaking, men show who they are, reveal actively their unique personal identities and thus make their appearance in the human world. (178–79)

Our deeds, according to Arendt, only partially define us. Without words, our actions may never be fully revealed, or completely understood. Knowing that words often stand for action, the combination of our deeds and words, or our words alone, add to our self–other conceptualizations and thus to the understanding of our position as subjects. This thinker highlights that our exchanges influence our cognition, our uniqueness as individuals, our relevance and place within our shared world. Regardless of time, place, or sociopolitical circumstances, Arendt's discussion of language knowingly and/or unknowingly touches on the area of semiotics, as well as arguments discussed throughout this chapter. Her experiences and conceptualizations provide us with an opening to this chapter's discussion on the sociopolitical weight of language. With a focus on migrancy, this chapter pays close attention to how dialogical processes shape and define migrants' condition(s) prior to, during, and following their relocation(s).

Conceptualizing Subjectivities within the Socio-Cognitive Significance of Language

In her book *The Multilingual Subject*, Claire Kramsch (2009) suggests that 'we become subjects and thus learn who we are and who we could be through our interactions with our environment; by means of the discourse and response of the other' (18). From such a claim we deduce that, by means of our everyday interactions, we respond, modify, incorporate, and propagate the interpretation of our realities. In other words, we conceptualize the fluidity of our place within the space that Umberto Eco calls 'the universe of our culture'. Kramsch expands her argument on language and subjectivity by stating that as subjects we have 'a responsibility to signify, that is to use and interpret signs, to respond and "reaccentuate" signs, to pass judgment and to make moral decisions' (Bakhtin 1981: 87, cited in Kramsch 2009: 18).

In Kramsch's original source, *The Dialogic Imagination*, Mikhail Bakhtin (1981) argues that internal or external dialogue between two people, or between someone's earlier and later self, is impossible without our willingness and ability to reinterpret or reaccentuate existing belief systems (9, 43). According to Bakhtin, only through such modifications and the rejection of canonized discourse[3] may we 'come-into-consciousness'.[4] By doing so, he continues, we become free from the persuasive authority that exists within the globalized or societal scale (5, 341–42, 385–86). Through such a semiotic lens, we understand that when individuals interact with one another, they are influenced by the 'multilingualism' that becomes knowingly and unknowingly integrated within their speech. In Bakhtin's terms, such multilingualism is unrelated to speakers' ability to interact in more than one language or linguistic code. Instead, as Bakhtin suggests, it is formed and informed by the combination of voices that have been reaccentuated, incorporated—and eventually transmitted—by its speakers.

The complexity and meaning of our day-to-day interactions are stressed throughout Bakhtin's work. As claimed by this semiotician, when we speak, we do not necessarily repeat the words of others. Instead, we appropriate the authority transcended through language by giving language our own meanings or, borrowing from Bakhtin's words, our own 'accents'. Looking through a semiotic lens, we understand that by conceptualizing others' significations and discourse to reflect our situation, intention, and style, we knowingly and unknowingly become influenced by their words (Bakhtin 1981: 309–10, 312, 315–16). Finding meaning within, while becoming influenced by a discourse that predates and surrounds us, suggests Derrida, is not strictly a conscious act. In line with psychoanalytic thought, through the process of incorporation, the belief systems that surround us knowingly and unknowingly affect the interpretation of our interconnected worlds. Specifically, they weigh in on our understanding of the sociocultural, political, and psycho-emotional realities that define while becoming part of us.

Along such lines, in her interpretation of Derrida's (1996) *Monolingualism of the Other*, Aparna Mishra Tarc (2015) highlights how, for Derrida, infants become positioned within pre-existing realities and frameworks of thinking and experiencing. She suggests that when Derrida claims 'I only speak one language, but the language is not mine', he points to the Other's influence or mark on our conceptualizations and ways of seeing the world. Mishra Tarc situates Derrida's argument within the Oedipal scene (9) and, along Lacan's lines, the child's initiation into language. Agreeing with Derrida, she suggests that cognition and thinking occur in relation to the symbolic register—and psychic imprint—we have internalized since infancy. Specifically, she claims, 'we depend on our internal register to think, speak and communicate ourselves in relation and with judgment to others and the world' (8–9).

Mishra Tarc addresses such a mark or imprint as a cultural 'colonization' of what is deemed normative and acceptable. She points to how society's ideas of what is considered civilized versus uncivilized affect the development of the individual's inner reality and how one makes sense of the surrounding world. Along Derrida's lines, the enunciation of a word is never considered the speaker's own. Instead, their words become full or partial projections of the symbolic law: introjected belief systems, alienating opinions of morality and immorality, as well as overall lasting literacies that always come from the Other (7).

A close reading of the discussions offered by Arendt and their relation to those of Bakhtin, Kramsch, and Mishra Tarc reminds us how an internalized language has the interconnected function of influencing while becoming influenced by us. Whether written, spoken, or signed, our symbolic code of meanings marks how we understand, shape, and define our social and inner worlds. A lived language perceptively and inadvertently imprints the way we see our complex realities, relate to the Other, and (mis)understand our past and present selves. By means of this shared and yet personal phenomenon, we become positioned within a socially constructed discourse and conceptualize the fluidity of our subjectivities and sense of self. Throughout the course of our lives, our sense of being becomes constructed, deconstructed, and reconstructed through the juxtaposition of our experiences and interactions with others. As discussed thus far, such a non-stable sense of being is also driven by

DIALOGIC ENCOUNTERS

the admixture of language's opposing tensions: 1) the one of change that fosters the realization of our cognitive and socio-affective growth, and 2) the one that canonizes and assimilates the oppressing, pre-existing frameworks we knowingly and unknowingly internalize as our own.

Comprehending our language's influential nature and link to our subjectivity is key to this section of the book. This chapter looks at how surrounding belief systems and resulting behaviours have short- and long-lasting consequences affecting individuals' lives. Following our discussion of the link between language and our ability to reason, this chapter looks at how this web of language influences our lives, while potentially inhibiting or restricting our growth as subjects. It studies how our code may condition, limit, or infringe upon our understandings, sense of morals, empathy, and ability to think in place of the Other. Following a discussion of how the linguistic web that surrounds us has an inevitable influence on our social and inner worlds, this chapter turns our attention to the dichotomized effects of language. It studies how belief systems and resulting behaviours affect families' and young individuals' pre- and post-migration experiences, and how such experiences may have short- and long-term effects on newcomers' adjustments and sense of belonging.

The Influential Meaning of our Symbolic Code

In a televised 1964 interview that aired on West German television, Hannah Arendt reflected on her experiences in relation to her work in political sciences. In her conversation with the German journalist Günter Gaus, Arendt stressed language's implication in her ability to examine the events that led to, occurred during, and followed the Shoah. While discussing her need to conceptualize and communicate the private and shared history that guided her reasoning and academic focus, Arendt provided her audience with a discerning representation of her theory.

During this interview, Arendt, together with Gauss, addressed the prevailing behaviours in Germany following the war. In the transcript published in *The Portable Hannah Arendt*, both speakers claimed that while some German civilians were trying to come to terms with the extent of the devastation that had affected millions of people's lives, others were driven by a premature need for normalcy (15). One may assume that the latter was grounded in civilians' response to the stress and tiredness of an ongoing war. For some, their desire to

CHILD AND ADOLESCENT MIGRATION, MENTAL HEALTH, AND LANGUAGE

leave the past behind reflected their willingness to heal and return to a peaceful life. Yet their need to forget and return to normalcy may also have been rooted in retrospective feelings associated with compliance.

Along such lines, Levi (1989) suggests that in Germany, civilians' post-war amnesia was associated with their innermost necessity to forget the actions of 'most Germans of the time' (Levi, cited in Agamben 1999: 95). Reinforcing Levi's claim, Agamben adds that, following the war, people's need for silence was directly linked to guilt—over 'not having had the courage to speak, to bear witness to what they could not not have seen' (Agamben 1999: 95). Such a feeling, he continues, which permeated people's lives, was highlighted following the war: once the crisis, inhumanity, and extensive damage caused by the Holocaust were brought to an unquestionable light. Yet when referring to the German people, Arendt stressed: 'they were not all murderers. There were people who fell into their own trap ... Nor did they desire what came later' (Baehr 2000: 14).

Following the war, the national and international focus on and discussion of the genocide created a belated space for civilian guilt. For many, this response was born from realizing that they were accomplices through their inaction and silence. Above the fear of resisting the tyranny that ruled Germany, and beyond a need for self-preservation, civilians' silence resulted from the acceptance and internalization of dominant views. Such conscious and unconscious acts justified their compliance and disregard or indifference towards the suffering and murder of millions of innocent people.

Relevant to this discussion, in *Frames of War: When Is Life Grievable?* Judith Butler (2009) discusses how interpretative frameworks regulate our emotions and moral responsiveness to events. She argues that such responsiveness is influenced by individuals' interpretation of specific lives as valuable or non-valuable, and therefore worthy or unworthy of grief (41). Butler's publication refers directly to Western, post 9/11 attitudes, and the United States' ongoing intervention in the Middle East. Yet her argument covers a more generalized phenomenon. Her words apply to most—if not all—past and present instances involving acts of war, persecution, and/or oppression. Butler's argument may easily be taken a step further by understanding that it is not limited to instances of war, particular places, or, to a greater or lesser scale, to specific historical times. Butler's discourse is also relevant to our current realities, to instances of systemic discrimination, and to the unjust treatment to which ethnic, racial, gender, religious, and/or linguistic minorities are subjected.

DIALOGIC ENCOUNTERS

Likewise, even though Arendt's interview addresses a reality that corresponds to a not-so-distant past, it seems fitting to link her recollections and rationalization to injustices inflicting our present-day world. Specific to the area of migration, Arendt's, Levi's, Agamben's and Butler's assertions create a space for us to consider the injustices individuals often encounter before their relocation: when fleeing injustice, violence, discrimination, and/or persecution. Their arguments also point to the ongoing challenges many migrant communities encounter while in transit and in host countries.

The Ethos of Violence and Why It Matters to this Chapter's Discussion

In her book *How Dare the Sun Rise: Memoirs of a War Child*, Sandra Uwiringiyimana shares the extreme consequences of the internalization and transmissibility of oppressive conceptualizations. Years following her migration as a child, and while recalling her private and shared histories in Congo, Africa, Uwiringiyimana (2017) narrates:

> There are hundreds of different tribes in Congo. My people, the Banyamulenge, have long been discriminated against and targeted in the region. Much of our early history is from word of mouth. I learned about it over the years from my parents ... They explained that in the late 1800s, many members of my tribe began moving from their native Rwanda to the mountains of South Kivu, a Congolese province. The tribe migrated for several reasons, including civil war and discrimination at home ... My tribe's migration came amid the time of European colonialism ... Eventually, in 1960, the Congolese won a bloody battle for independence from Belgium. But the region was left deeply unstable, and civil wars raged. My people in South Kivu ran into political problems because they lived in a Congolese province but spoke a language of their native Rwanda. My people looked different, sounded different. They tried to keep to themselves. And so they were foreigners ... Different groups vying for power would come after my people ... and chaos reigned ... My parents grew up amid these conflicts. (16–17)

Uwiringiyimana traces her people's history of cumulative oppression and its effects on her own experiences as a child:

> In June 2004, the tensions toward my people escalated quickly. The Congolese kids at school were calling me Rwandan all the time, dubbing me a foreigner,

repeating what they had heard at home. 'You are Rwandan' they would yell. I would give them my standard reply: 'I'm not. I've never been there.' (60)

Such a rise in tensions, she continues, led to her eventual need to flee from Uvira.[5] However, instead of providing a sense of safety, their escape increased the violence to which she, along with members of her immediate family, was exposed:

> My parents ... said we needed to leave immediately. My dad asked our neighbours—who were not members of our tribe and did not need to flee— to get an urgent message to [my siblings] Chris and Adele to leave school and head for the mountains to stay with our grandparents ... Weaving through the streets of Uvira, we watched people frantically trying to get out of the city ... suddenly we were stopped at a checkpoint, or rather, an ambush. A blockade of chairs, benches, and tables lay across the road, and men stood there with guns, forcing us to stop. On the side of the road, a mob of angry Congolese people stood—men, women and children— ... They carried machetes, knives and rifles ... The crowd rushed toward us and began shaking the minivan ... People reached in trying to grab us ... I had known that many Congolese people disliked us, but I had never seen such hate on people's faces. Even little kids were shaking the van angrily. Why are these kids so furious? I thought. They don't even know us ... We were completely exposed, with no way out. We must have sat there for almost an hour, waiting to die. We couldn't jump into the mob ... but then, a miracle: an angel appeared ... A young Congolese man ... [saved us] ... he managed to wedge himself into the car. People didn't try to fight him since he was Congolese. (62–63, 65)

Uwiringiyimana provides us with an understanding of how the linguistic web that shapes while containing thinkers' interactive worlds, structures a sense of personal and shared reason and morality. In *How Dare the Sun Rise*, we see how language propagates the justification for these sorts of acts. Such a problem is not particular to one place or time. Throughout the recorded history of humankind, marginalized groups have become targets of a wide range of physical and psycho-emotional aggressions. As noted earlier, both perpetrators and those who are complacent are implicated. When individuals and families are persecuted and cannot rely on their own governments for justice and safety, applying for international protection as asylum seekers becomes a hopeful solution to the immeasurable threat and injustices they experience.

The 1951 Refugee Convention has defined a refugee as someone who:

> owing to a well-founded fear of being persecuted for reasons of race, religion, nationality, membership of a particular social group or political opinion, is outside of the country of his nationality, and is unable to, or owing to such fear, unwilling to avail himself of the protection of that country. (UNHCR, cited in Juneau & Rubin 2014: para. 2)

As seen with Uwiringiyimana and her family, asylum is granted to those from war-torn countries or individuals who can demonstrate credible or reasonable fears of persecution based on religion, race, nationality, membership of a social group, or political opinion (Rosenblum 2015: 1, 7). The problem that asylum seekers often encounter is that not everyone is able to offer concrete evidence of persecution. Hence, even if individuals' and families' lives are in danger, if asylum seekers are threatened by circumstances that rest outside the guidelines of persecution, they do not meet the necessary criteria for international protection.[6] In the existence of such barriers, we can see how legal or approved international relocations may prove to be impossible for many individuals whose lives are, in fact, threatened.

Dominant Ideological Beliefs, Migration, and Receiving Countries

Unfortunately, Uwiringiyimana's difficulties did not end when she fled her childhood home in Africa. Nor did they end with her relocation to America as a refugee. While in Africa, she and her family were victims of genocide. In the United States, however, following her resettlement (118), this writer describes being exposed to 'a more subtle violence' and 'a different type of warzone' (171). Such hostility, she states, becomes noticeable through the media, movies, and music (168–71, 182, 208). Her experience of 'soft' violence affected her existential experiences.[7] The attitudes and behaviours that encompassed her American reality influenced her subject position as a linguistic and visible minority and a refugee. When studying the psycho-emotional effects of forced relocations across transit and destination countries, we must first consider the link between receiving systems and attitudes towards newcomers. As briefly mentioned, newcomers' known and unknown, imaginable and unimaginable experiences do not always end the moment they escape the confines of their countries of origin. In resettlement countries, the sudden change in migrants' and refugees' subject position, combined with symbolic, systemic, and sometimes physical violence, become concerning factors impacting newcomers' experiences. These may affect newcomers' sense of safety, short- and long-term adjustment, and emotional well-being.

The challenges present within receiving countries are articulated well by Charles Simic (1999) when he states:

> It's hard for people who have never experienced it, to truly grasp what it means to lack proper documents ... I remember standing in endless lines in Paris at police headquarters to receive or renew resident permits ... We'd wait all day only to discover that the rules had changed since the last time ... we'd be listening to someone at the next window trying to convey in poor French how the family's house had burned, how they'd left in a hurry with only one small suitcase, and so on, to which the official would shrug his shoulders and proceed to inform them that unless the documents were produced promptly, the resident permit would be denied ... [immigration officials] suspected us of not being what we claimed to be. No one likes refugees. The ambiguous status of being called a DP [displaced person] made it even worse. (121–23)

Even though Simic's experience took place in 1945, the desperation to 'flee evil with no idea where they were running to' (120), combined with migrants' powerlessness and confounding encounters with receiving systems, is often experienced to this date. In today's global era of increased displacements, migrants, refugees, and asylum seekers from Latin America, the Caribbean Islands, as well as Asian, African, and East European states (Hodes et al. 2018: 389, 397), are crossing international borders in extraordinary numbers.[8] Hence, transit states and countries sought out as safer and more affluent destinations have been overwhelmed with the unforeseen influx of despairing arrivals.[9]

Countries' response to urgent, global challenges involving wars, violence, persecution, extreme poverty, environmental disasters, and health crises vary across regions and time. Yet factors that determine destination countries' receiving systems, as well as their increase or decrease in immigration and refugee quotas, result from an admixture of economic concerns and countries' nationalist sentiments. The financial costs associated with migrants' settlement and newcomers' health, psychological, social, and educational needs may become

DIALOGIC ENCOUNTERS

deterrents to countries opening their borders. Historically, decisions to increase or limit movements have also been affected by nationalist sentiments (Palmer 1976: 488). Such sentiments and the resulting policies are often entangled with questions of race and racism, xenophobia, and fears of radicalism.

Immigration, Racialization, and Racism

Historically, portraying immigrants as sources of physical or racial contamination have [*sic*] been effective in determining which borders should be open to whom, and who the outsiders are. These discourses have been used to target Others ... in immigration policies (Kendall 2008; Yeoh and Kong 2012; Day 2016). (Cited in Ang, Ho & Yeoh 2022: 587)

Ideological webs that at times are canonized, while at others altered through further dialogical constructions, deconstructions, and reconstructions, shape how individuals become perceived and positioned. Added to traditional racism, which is clear, intended, and therefore part of a conscious discourse, is the modern or new form. In the latter, dialogical, overtly racist influences are indiscernible and almost hidden from those who become part of its propagation. The challenge with this new or modern racism is that it forms part of a subtle everyday discourse. It becomes, as highlighted by Ang, Ho, and Yeoh (2022), 'racism without [apparent] racists' (587). It seems natural and rooted in an ostensible common sense. This form of racism may not only evade speakers' awareness, but it has also evolved 'beyond the traditional perspective of biological superiority and colour to discriminate against cultures, religions and class' (587). This racism does not seem founded on the belief of racial superiority. Instead, it seems founded on logic or reason. If we take Germany as an example, we note that in response to the 2015 Syrian War, Germany exercised an open-door policy to immigration.[10] Unfortunately, this humanitarian course of action only lasted three years. By 2018, following terrorist attacks on its home soil, opposition within its government, and anti-immigration concerns voiced by its citizens, Germany's progressive policy became curtailed (Dockery 2017: n.p.). Here we note that the country's quota restriction does not seem to be rooted in traditional racism. Instead, it was seemingly linked to its citizens' safety and an apparent common sense.

Living in Canada, a neighbouring country that comes to mind when analysing the connection between thought, discrimination, and action, is the United

States. Among the many instances we may highlight is the implementation of Title 42. In March 2020, during the Covid-19 outbreak, under the pretence of health-crisis management, the Trump administration, with the support of its Center for Disease Control, enacted a policy that allowed for immigration officials to 'automatically expel almost all undocumented migrants seeking entry, bypassing normal immigration laws and protections' (BBC 2022: para. 5). With the enactment of Title 42, accompanied minors and their families seeking asylum from countries such as Honduras, Haiti, El Salvador, Guatemala, and Nicaragua, and from southern Mexican states, were immediately deported with no opportunity for fair trial. Title 42 has not only affected recent arrivals. This border policy has also impacted those who had already crossed and were awaiting hearings. Hence, on the US side of the US–Mexico border, asylum seekers who were detained before March 2020 have been given the option to either separate from their children, or remain together as family units.[11] If choosing the latter, many parents were forced to waive their children's right to parole. Waiving such a right implied that children could be held in detention with their parents under carceral conditions for longer than twenty days.[12]

As claimed by *BBC News*, under the Biden administration, a shift towards more humanitarian approaches to illegal entries seems to be taking place in the United States. Following his election, Biden has halted the construction of the notorious USA–Mexico wall. Even though Title 42 remains in place until 'the spread of non-citizens stops being a "serious danger" to public health' (para. 8), his current administration has pledged to reform its immigration laws. Unlike his predecessor, Biden is not refusing entry to unaccompanied minors. He is also allowing entry to 'some' families. In addition, as mandated by US anti-trafficking laws, the country has been transferring most immigrant children to shelters overseen by the government. This is, without a doubt, a step in the right direction. Yet, as pointed out by Amnesty International, regardless of Biden's changes, the United States should continue to improve its practices when addressing the challenges encountered at its southern borders (BBC 2022: para. 6).

As the media reduces its focus on Covid-19, the everchanging nature of viruses, and how vaccination, mask mandates, and travel restrictions may affect different aspects of people's lives, attention has been partially shifted to the war in Eastern Europe and the humanitarian response to the people of Ukraine. In the Western hemisphere, the reaction to the Ukrainian crisis stands in stark contrast to the response to asylum seekers from Latin American, Africa, and the Middle East. Biden's administration is not alone in its pledge to a stream-lined process to welcome Ukrainians to the United States (Homeland Security 2022). Countries across Europe and around the world are also helping indi-viduals trying to flee from Russia's most recent aggression. What matters most to this section's discussion is the fact that the media and politicians' response to this crisis stands in stark contrast to previous responses involving racialized refugees of Hispanic, Caribbean, African, or Middle Eastern descent.

Returning to Canada, an example of racialization and bias is seen in the divisive, and later welcoming, comments made by the Premier of Ontario. On 18 October 2021, while addressing migration and the skilled labour shortage in the province, Doug Ford addressed viewers and newcomers to the province by stating: 'You come here like every other new Canadian. You work your tail off … If you think you're coming to collect the dole [unemployment benefits] and sit around, it's not going to happen. Go somewhere else' (Neufeld 2021: para. 3). Yet this same premier offered a very different rhetoric six months later, when he pledged support for Ukrainian families. Making his announce-ment in Etobicoke, his home city, Ford declared: 'This is where I grew up. I was born here and have a lot of Ukrainian friends … They've been absolutely outstanding—literally given the shirt off their backs. We're going to be there to support them.' In that same interview, Ford announced substantial financial support from the province of Ontario, which, he continued, would see more than 40,000 refugees in the coming months (Tsekouras 2022: paras 2–3).

At this point of our discussion, it is essential to note that this shift in perspectives does not, by any means, deny the seriousness of the current war crimes taking place in Ukraine. Nor is it meant to criticize the international help that is needed for Ukrainian women, children, and elder men fleeing their homeland (Taub 2022). Instead, this argument draws attention to racist atti-tudes at the core of immigration rhetoric. It is a focus on how racism knowingly and unknowingly infiltrates societies, either helping or marginalizing, includ-ing or othering groups of migrants and 'would-be migrants' attempting to flee from unsustainable, life-threatening conditions that are directly and irrevoca-bly affecting their lives.

When studying immigration, racism, and racialization, it becomes appar-ent that hegemonic relations between dominant and migrant groups are not reduced to white–other binaries. In 'Migration and new racism beyond colour and the "West"', Ang, Ho, and Yeoh (2022), when drawing attention to current shifts in migration movements, examine interethnic encounters and co-ethnic othering within host Asian countries. They stress how in today's era of increasing transnational movements, many emigrants, instead of relocating to traditionally white, Western countries, try re-establishing themselves in destination countries not composed of white dominant groups. In such host countries, marginalization of migrants is not necessarily—or solely—based on cultural differences. Instead, it is founded on migrants' perceived uprootedness (588).

Ang et al. draw attention to how today's new racism has made its unwelcome appearance through Covid-19. Their publication focuses on anti-Chinese rhetoric and how Chinese individuals have been linked to the virus and made victims of racism within their country of migration:

> in Singapore, mainland Chinese businesses and Chinese nationals have reported being shunned and the latter verbally abused while an online petition urging the Singaporean government to ban travel from China gathered 125,000 signatures (Lee and Loke 2020; Chia and Yong 2020). In South Korea, restaurant owners have displayed 'no Chinese allowed' signs while Japanese Twitter users circulated the hashtag #ChineseDontComeToJapan (Della Cava and Lam 2020). (Cited in Ang, Ho & Yeoh 2022: 587)

This focus on the evolution of racism beyond the perspective of racial superiority forces scholars to move away from the assumption that racialization and racism mostly take place among individuals of diverse ethnic backgrounds and languages (586).

Historical Responses to the Exponential Increase in Transnational Movements

Changes in governments' response to immigration and refugee quotas, along with amendments and strategies that restrict, criminalize, and punish illegal entries, have been common across developed countries. To take Canada as an example—this country has not always been known for its multiculturalist policies and society, or for its compassionate approach to ongoing global humanitarian crises. During the nineteenth and twentieth centuries, Canada refused entry to many individuals who were poor, ill, and disabled. Its government

DIALOGIC ENCOUNTERS

also opposed entry by individuals and/or family units immigrating from select geographical regions. Canada's policies discouraged immigration from particular groups, especially those of non-Christian and non-Northern European backgrounds. Even though Canada's government claimed that such decisions were taken because accepting non-economic migrants would drain the country's economic system, immigration laws were influenced by citizens' attitudes and ideas regarding specific ethnic minorities, and/or the places from which would-be migrants came.

As seen in the United States, Canada's former geographic selection was embedded in the determination of applicants' perceived similarities to the Canadian culture. These included likenesses in belief systems and ways of life, and hence newcomers' presumed ability to better integrate into the host country's culture and sociological composition (Palmer 1997: 85–86). In Canada, attitudes towards migrants shifted during World War II. During this period, the country's willingness to welcome newcomers was influenced by international agreements, belief systems, Canada's demographics, and its labour market needs. While such positive change increased the rate of migrants, who were mostly coming from Europe, a negative shift was seen during the Cold War, when anti-communist sentiments discouraged entry to migrants with ties to the Soviet Union (Cheatham & Roy, n.d., para. 4).

Geographic restrictionism ended in Canada in 1967 with the introduction of the point-based approach to immigration. This system, which is in use to this date, led to an increase in the number of migrants relocating from a much wider range of places, including Africa, Latin America, the Caribbean, and Asia (para. 5). As with Canada, countries such as the United States, the United Kingdom, Australia, New Zealand, and Japan have also adopted a point-based approach. With this system, factors such as education level, wealth, host-language fluency, and existing job offers in receiving countries are considered when providing a score to potential migrants. With this approach to immigration, only those who score above a particular threshold are eligible for legal entry to a desirable country (Rosenblum 2015: 2).

While the focus on migrants' backgrounds seemingly came to a halt, a different sort of challenge remained in place: Unless applicants are financially stable, satisfy specified host-language fluency, and meet the destination country's labour needs, they are deemed unqualified. Some displaced families and individuals who live in terror of being persecuted may apply for international protection as asylum seekers. Yet the greatest challenge rests on the fact that, regardless of individuals' and families' dire reasons to relocate, not all claimants are eligible for—or have enough proof to claim—international protection.

For children and adolescents, the distinctions between accompanied and unaccompanied minors, legal and illegal migrants, and individuals seeking international protection as refugees have direct consequences on the treatment and support individuals may receive following their departure from their country of origin. Emigrants who qualify and pass screening processes are granted the freedom to relocate through safe, legal means. Yet, as argued thus far, immigrating through legal channels is not within reach for most of those who try. Regardless of age, motivation, and absence of criminal records, many would-be migrants are considered unqualified and denied passage to safer destinations. Through the point system, in order to relocate legally as migrants, applicants need to prove that they are economically stable, they speak at least one of the official languages of the country to which they intend to migrate, and their work or profession is in demand. Likewise, to apply as refugees, claimants need evidence of persecution. In other words, extreme poverty, as an example, is not a sufficient reason for approval. This is especially the case if applicants do not hold a desired profession, have had no or limited access to an education, and are not fluent in at least one of the official languages spoken in the destination country.

As we focus on families and children under the age of eighteen, it is fitting to address the principles proclaimed in the United Nations Convention of the Rights of the Child (UNCRC). Agreed upon by 194 countries, including Canada, these principles state that children's physical, mental, spiritual, moral, social, and educational development should always be protected. Hence, when minors' development and overall rights are threatened in their home country, by conditions such as extreme poverty and starvation, nations that signed such a humanitarian agreement should consider offering viable solutions. Famine and devastation across the globe are widespread. Yet regardless of its devastating threat to children's lives, living in extreme poverty does not suffice for a legal relocation. At least in part, this truth explains why, out of desperation and an unrelenting need for physical, psychological, and emotional survival, people risk their lives and, at times, the lives of their loved ones, by engaging in clandestine border crossings.[13]

Conclusion

This chapter brought together the complexity of migrants' experiences. It focused on the intricate connection between immigration, racialization, and racism, and studied how discourses at the national and international scale have direct effects on families and individuals. It also looked at how intended and unintended discourses may give way to push factors and to the experiences migrants may endure while in transit and following their migration(s). As argued throughout this chapter, we are surrounded, formed, and informed by the symbolic code of meanings that influence and engulf the intricacy of our social experiences. Through dialogic processes we become positioned within the sociocultural and political webs that mark our self–other relations and, by extension, our sense of self. This chapter examined how the propagation of ideas, directly and indirectly, knowingly and unknowingly, affects our lives. It stressed how we are not only recipients but also actors in all dialogic exchanges. As outlined by Arendt, with our own words and with our silences, we engage and corroborate in constructions that either embrace or marginalize the Other.

Chapter 1 therefore laid the grounds for an understanding of the varying difficulties many documented and undocumented migrants experience in relation to dominant belief systems. It highlighted how racialization and racism, xenophobia, and fear of radicalism within home, destination, and transit countries affect perceptions of international crises and, by extension, countries' willingness to help. It brought attention to the manner in which nationalist sentiments influence immigration policies, receiving systems, and thus the treatment families and individuals receive during and following their relocations. Equally importantly, this chapter zeroed in on how we knowingly and unknowingly partake in others' traumas—how our shared and personal interactions may directly and indirectly add to migrants' cumulative crises through the propagation of new and/or old forms of racism and the enactment of laws that determine migrants' pre- and post-relocation experiences. It created a space for the subsequent chapter's attention to how immigration policies and receiving systems further exacerbate the precariousness of minors' condition prior to, during, and following their attempt at relocation. Centred on this volume's focus on child and adolescents' mental health, Chapter 2 examines the danger of illegal crossings and how common receiving systems for irregular migrants and asylum seekers add to their cumulative crises.

2 Migration and Trauma: Defining the Problem of Child and Adolescent Transnational Relocations

My parents belonged to a Pentecostal church in Brooklyn called Evangelical Crusade of Fishers of Men, which was very much involved with refugee work. So on Sunday afternoons after church, we would go and visit many refugees in confinement at the Brooklyn Navy Yard detention center. We would go to talk to them and pray with them, listen to their complaints, and, most important, get the names of relatives to contact on their behalf. After looking into their eyes and holding their hands, watching them cry and fully acknowledging once more how much they had sacrificed to come to the United States, I never understood why the children at school would shout their fate at us as a curse: 'Get back on your banana boats, you dirty Haitians!'

(Danticat 2000: 41)

In the book *Becoming American: Personal Essays by First Generation Immigrant Women*, Edwidge Danticat shares her remembered experiences as a twelve-year-old new migrant residing in the United States. She recalls how, after fleeing from Haiti's dictatorship, she and her family immigrated to Brooklyn, New York in 1981. According to Danticat, instances of open racism in this host country were due, at least in part, to the emergence of AIDS— specifically, to the manner in which the media linked the disease to homosexuals, haemophiliacs, heroin addicts, and Haitians (41). Misguided dominant beliefs and resulting actions increased the writer's experience of marginalization. According to this Haitian writer, the recurrent marginalization she experienced within her host country situated a feeling 'Baudelaire called

MIGRATION AND TRAUMA

the grand malaise, secretly relishing the role of permanent outsider, never expecting to belong' (44).

This book's first chapter stressed how dominant belief systems feed into hegemonic relations by targeting and discriminating against specific groups. When studying minors' experiences, we could concur that racialization and racism are not only experienced at schools, in neighbourhoods, and for adolescents and adults, within workplaces. Discrimination based on countries of origin and race are also evident in countries' immigration policies and their receiving systems. With that in mind, this chapter turns readers' attention to the way nationalist sentiments affect the treatment minors and families receive within transit and destination countries. With a focus on irregular relocations, this chapter aims in furthering our previous discussion by establishing the links between receiving systems, minors' short- and long-term cumulative crises, and mental health.

Illegal Crossings, Families, and Unaccompanied Minors

Transit and destination countries' responses to unplanned and illegal entries vary across time and place. Currently, in regions surrounding Ukraine and in Eastern Europe, there are humanitarian corridors enabling safe passage to those desperately fleeing from danger. Yet, as often seen in places like Northern Mexico and at coastal points of entry to Europe, unauthorized arrivals, regardless of the dire conditions that lead to their need to relocate, are either refused entry or are forced to encamp in makeshift settlements or government-run camps. Makeshift and government-run settlements are not the only response to unexpected entries. Countries such as Australia, the United Kingdom, Canada, Japan, and the United States hold or detain some illegal entrants. In these enclosed, carceral environments, illegal entrants who are considered flight risks or labelled as potentially dangerous are held while awaiting trials, or until their identification is confirmed.

Often, the austerity migrants encounter while in transit is directly linked to racism and the way illegal migration is criminalized. Too often, undocumented entrants are not seen as desperate individuals unable to rely on legal means to migrate. Instead, they are perceived as offenders who infiltrate host countries with criminal intentions. The problem is that while this may be true for some crossers, it is not the case for everyone.

27

A Brief Look into Europe's Border Management System

In Europe, concerns over the increasing number of asylum seekers arriving from other continents by sea, growing anti-Islamic fears, xenophobia, and anti-migrant opposition from the extreme right have led to the development of a hotspot system within the continent's external borders. As seen in Italy and Greece, these centres are part of a border management system that is meant to register, control, and contain unexpected arrivals (Tazzioli 2017: 2765). Many migrants landing on the Greek and Italian shores intend to seek asylum in other countries within Europe. Since Greece and Italy are located at the continent's external borders, they are seen by newcomers as transit zones.[1] These EU receiving states have the responsibility to identify all migrants (2765). Thus, upon arrival, irregular migrants are fingerprinted by authorities, and their information, including country of origin and biometric data, is entered into a common system known as the Eurodac database. The gathering of their personal information, including fingerprints, may occur while individuals are still detained in vessels, at ports after they have been allowed to disembark, or in hotspot facilities (2770).

In Greece, as in Italy, migrants whose applications are approved are streamlined to specific countries within Europe.[2] Yet as Tazzioli claims, since individual circumstances are barely considered, most applicants are denied asylum (2769). While going through the registration process, although many are asked to provide information on the reason(s) for their irregular migration, conclusions on immediate rejections or decisions to consider migrants' applications for asylum are commonly based on the country from which individuals emigrated (2768).[3] Protocol and processing times in Italy and Greece range from two to three weeks to over a year.[4] In Italy, individuals considered for protection are transferred to hosting centres to wait for their asylum claims to be processed, and those considered inadmissible are either taken to detention centres or given decrees of expulsion (2769). In Greece, individuals deemed inadmissible are commonly rerouted back to Turkey (2773).[5] In Italy, meanwhile, those rejected are expected to leave the country by their own means. In Italy, if migrants who have been processed and rendered inadmissible attempt to move further into Europe, their journey is obstructed at the northern borders. In this case, inadmissible migrants caught trying to cross Italian borders are sent to detention centres in the south of Italy (2772). Since illegal migrants

MIGRATION AND TRAUMA

are commonly unable to move back to their country of origin, their vulnerable condition worsens as they form part of the country's underpaid, exploited, and disposable labour (2769).

Makeshift Camps across Europe

Following the initial stages of arrival, since most international protection applications are rejected, many migrants are either at risk of becoming repatriated or find themselves travelling within the strict borders of an unwelcoming receiving country. In the latter case, these men, women, and children who have been labelled as inadmissible, and hence suspended from further movement across Europe, resourcefully construct makeshift camps. Unlike government-run camps, these provisional spaces are created and run by displaced migrants seeking temporary shelter. Commonly, such developments are erected in urban areas at 'bottlenecks' near a border where a restriction of further movement is in place (Katz 2016: 17–18). Although those considered 'undesirable' may recover their agency in makeshift camps, they remain socially, culturally, and linguistically isolated (18). Their conditions are unsanitary, inadequate, and frequently demolished or 'bulldozed' by local authorities. Having nowhere else to go, unsuccessful asylum seekers are then forced to move once again to build another unofficial camp at a nearby location (18–19).

Unsuccessful asylum seekers who enter Europe's receiving system are typically left to their own means. Having been denied international protection, individuals of all ages, genders, physical abilities, and health and psychological conditions are left unsheltered, on the repeated move, and afraid of becoming (re)detained. Even though NGO activists and volunteers from neighbouring communities often support inhabitants of makeshift camps (18), rejected migrants inevitably find themselves consumed by their homelessness as well as their financial and health-related needs. Children sheltered by their parents in makeshift spaces have no access to education. Along with their families, they are marginalized and left unprotected regardless of hunger, anxieties, and potential short- and/or long-term medical and mental health concerns. Along with their parents, children are exposed to cumulative stressors that stem from their extreme condition: one that often involves the effects of symbolic and physical violence. Theirs is an unsustainable reality marked by a continuous need for survival, a vulnerability to crime, and the discernible possibility of exploitation.

Challenges of Being on the Move

Traumas not only stem from conditions that force refugees to leave their homes. Many become traumatized at migrant camps, where they are often exposed to sexual harassment, rape, and physical abuse. Such incidents often become compounded with food insecurity and unsanitary living conditions, as well as their forced confinement and stateless condition—all of which has the potential to exacerbate or complicate PTSD symptoms (McGregor, Melvin & Newman 2015: 5–7). In Europe, the stress that irregular migrants endure is cumulative. Aside from the terrifying conditions lived before and during their journey to Europe and at hotspots and detention centres, individuals experience poor living conditions and interrupted health services. For most migrants, their condition worsens following their release. When migrants' applications for asylum are unsuccessful, the open insecurity that defines their condition as illegal foreigners dampens their sense of hope for a promising future. For those who try to remain in Europe, their border entrapment, nomadism, and the everyday struggle to survive while on the move, combined with the lack of available services and resources, add to the precariousness of their experiences.

Within Europe's critical border zones, hotspots are places of containment. These are designed to control or interrupt people's secondary movements through Europe. Such interruption is achieved through registration, traceability, and control. When discussing Europe's system, Ajana (2013) argues:

> Control is not narrowed to disciplinary and direct monitoring of individuals. It refers to the potential localization and traceability of bodies across space and over time that can be made by a matching algorithm of the fingerprints stored in the Eurodac database with migrants' data that can be captured by police officers in any place in Europe. The government from a distance and via digital traceability is certainly an important aspect of the ways in which migrants are controlled. (Cited in Tazzioli 2017: 2767)

According to Tazzioli (2017), when added to detentions, the hotspot approach diverts irregular migrants' journeys into paths of confinement. As their movements are traced and restricted, individuals become trapped within a system that controls and limits their short- and long-term opportunities for what many may call a 'normal' life.

During their initial stages of arrival, irregular migrants are subjected to poor prevailing conditions. Aside from unsanitary and overcrowded conditions and food shortages, incidents of alcohol and drug use as well as violent outbursts are highly prevalent at hotspots and receiving centres.[6] As with most carceral environments, violence is also present at detention centres. Hence newcomers of all ages, physical abilities, and mental health concerns who are forced to remain in hotspots, receiving centres, or detention centres are commonly exposed to violence by either witnessing outbursts or becoming direct targets. Added to such concerns is the problem of inadequate or discontinued health and psychological services.

The phenomenon of unauthorized migrants constantly on the move has been part of Europe's temporary response to ongoing crises. As argued by Tazzioli (2017), dispersing and mobilizing migrants is a part of Europe's central plan to regain control of its borders (2765). This explains why government regulation over the movements of migrants, especially new arrivals, is common. Following their initial registration, individuals and entire families are often given short notices and limited information about their relocations. This, combined with repeated moves, affects the level and efficiency of medical and mental health services migrants receive. As argued in 'Primary care for refugees and newly arrived migrants in Europe' (van Loenen et al. 2017), the efficiency of healthcare services is infringed by 1) the usual absence of a common language and cultural connection between providers and patients, 2) the interruptions, brevity, and temporality of the treatments patients receive, and 3) the absence of data on patients' previous treatments, treatment plans, and medications (84–85).

Establishing a positive rapport with patients and being well informed on conditions are essential to the efficiency of rendered services. Migrants' medical and healthcare challenges are complex and multilayered. For those affected by traumas and/or ongoing stress, sharing their concerns helps improve their mental health. Yet such disclosure demands consistency, time, and patient–provider trust. Being constantly on the move, and thus changing locations and available healthcare workers, often with gaps in their health records, has an inevitable effect on the level and effectiveness of provided care. Following relocations, files are not transferred with patients. Hence many are required to re-explain their condition, concerns, medication, and treatment. Aside from being time-consuming and frustrating, these interruptions and the lack of a centralized input system may partially or fully annul healthcare professionals' previous efforts.

Bordering the United States: A Look into Conditions for Asylum Seekers in Tijuana

Makeshift encampments established by asylum seekers as a last resort are not only prominent across Europe and Africa. In the Americas, an exponential number of asylum seekers from impoverished countries, such as Honduras, Guatemala, El Salvador, and Haiti, have tried to cross to the United States from the north of Mexico. Through the implementation of immigration laws meant to deter irregular entries, places like Tijuana become a bottleneck for those hoping to cross. In such places people live in tents for undetermined periods of time. They encamp under detrimental conditions, without bathrooms or showers in areas that often become flooded by heavy rains. Families and individuals struggle to survive with a limited food supply and lack of clean, running water. At times, families are unable to return to their home country and some caregivers, out of desperation and unrelenting hope, try to increase their children's chances of survival by paying smugglers to help the children cross the border as unaccompanied minors. Those people make this difficult decision in the hope that their children's crossing will grant them an escape from hunger, violence, and death. As argued by Herrera (2021), parents' decision to smuggle their children is often linked to their need for them to escape 'from persecutors who have followed them to the border, or from extreme hunger' (para. 5). Smuggling minors is not always a decision parents can make, however—and thus many try to remain near the border as a family unit. Once again, the impossibility of returning to their home country and the prospect of adult deportation when crossing together keep families in this in-between state of toxic stress and constant danger.

Following an interview with a young woman camping in Tijuana, Herrera states:

> the possibility of being sent back to Honduras reads as a death sentence. She shows me the scars from torture at the hands of a powerful gang back at home that her family got on the wrong side of. Fearing further reprisals, [she] fled with her sister's children, a teenage nephew and teenage niece, as well as the niece's seven-month-old son. The children were in the process of claiming asylum in 2019, before the pandemic. Staying in Mexico, she says, was never a long-term solution and increasingly feels less tolerable … the family already tried to make a new life in the southern state of Oaxaca, but danger pursued them there, where her nephew was murdered. (paras 7–8)

MIGRATION AND TRAUMA

As in most makeshift camps, whether in the northern regions of Mexico, through Africa, or across the coastal regions of Europe, asylum seekers are exposed to unsanitary and unsafe conditions. They live in constant fear for their physical safety, and this, of course, may affect their short- and long-term psycho-emotional well-being.

Detention and Processing Centres

As mentioned briefly at the start of this chapter, in transit and receiving countries, added to makeshift and government-run hotspots and camps, there are detention and processing centres. These places hold individuals travelling alone, as well as family units. Most countries claim that detaining minors is a last resort. Yet the treatment minors receive depends on their status as accompanied or unaccompanied. If we take the United States as an example, once it is determined that a minor is unaccompanied, the receiving government first attempts to connect the child with relatives residing in their country of origin. If such contact is established and relatives can assume responsibility for the apprehended minor, the child is promptly repatriated. However, if no contact is successfully established, or if it is suspected that such reunification could potentially expose the child to human trafficking and exploitation, the child is not repatriated. In such cases, an attempt is made to locate relatives in the United States. If such a connection is established, and a relative or sponsor residing in the United States agrees to assume the care and financial responsibility of the child, the minor is released into the community until their immigration proceedings are finalized. If not repatriated or reunited with individuals residing in the United States, in compliance with the Flores Settlement Agreement, unaccompanied immigrant children are placed in non-secure state-licensed facilities, such as shelters, until their immigration proceedings conclude (Linton, Griffin & Shapiro 2017: 3, 5).[7]

Detaining children as part of family units becomes a breach of the UNCRC. That being said, unless family units are expatriated or minors are released to the community, children are commonly housed with their detained parent(s). As seen in Canada, the reasoning behind this observable breach is to keep families together (Global Detention Project 2018). Equally importantly, in the United States, a country that has not signed the international human rights treaty, immigration officials are expected to adhere to the Flores Settlement Agreement.

This agreement stipulates that unless parents waive their children's rights to be housed in non-secure facilities, no child should be detained in secure facilities for more than three to five days (Herman-Peck & Harrington 2018: 121). Nonetheless, as seen in 2015, if there is an influx of child arrivals, children may be detained in secure facilities for a maximum of twenty days (Herman-Peck & Harrington 2018: 120; Schweikart 2019: 1). This implies that following such a period, either: 1) family units are released into the community,[8] or 2) children are separated from adults while adults remain in detention. In the latter case, parents' or caregivers' detention extends until their immigration and/or criminal proceedings have concluded,[9] and a decision is made for them to remain in the country or be repatriated (Herman-Peck & Harrington 2018: 109, 123). When separated, and while proceedings are taking place, children are either placed in non-secure group/residential facilities, or in foster care facilities for dependent children (118). They may also be placed with relatives residing in the United States (125). The third option is housing family units in non-secure facilities until their proceedings conclude. The problem with this third option is the shortage of facilities that comply with conditions deemed acceptable according to the Flores Settlement Agreement (107, 109).

Child–adult Separations

As described thus far, unless minors are released into the community under supervision, receiving systems for illegal entries impact children's—and adults'—mental health. Like refugee camps, detention centres offer limited medical, dental, and psychological assistance. At detention or holding facilities, since individuals tend to be divided by gender, and since children are housed with mothers, minors who travel with their fathers or male caregivers become separated from them. Unfortunately, separations do not only occur post-migration, at detention centres, or against children's will. While many unaccompanied minors are children separated from their families during armed conflicts (Ensor 2016: 62), generalized violence, and/or natural disasters, not all unaccompanied children are orphaned, or forcefully separated from loved ones. Instead, some are willing individuals with agency (Sutterlüty & Tisdall 2019: 183). Often supported by their parents and loved ones, many minors decide to cross borders with smugglers in hopes of fleeing the extreme conditions threatening their lives. Under such circumstances, minors may become

MIGRATION AND TRAUMA

willing agents or unwilling victims of human trafficking. As argued by Linton, Griffin, and Shapiro (2017), with undocumented children, there is always the concern of human trafficking involving minors. Hence, due to an apparent concern over this conspicuous problem, when children travel with one or more adults who do not hold a biological relation with them, children become separated from adults and rendered unaccompanied (2).

Separations also occur while children and families are in transit. Pre-crossing separations may be by-products of reception systems. Such instances take place when individuals believe that their children will best succeed in claiming asylum when unaccompanied. In Tijuana, Mexico, for example, following the implementation of Title 42, many asylum seekers have halted their journey at the Mexican side of the border. They are living indefinitely in tents under dire conditions (BBC 2022: paras 2–4, 6). With Title 42, federal officials in the USA were granted the power to immediately deport asylum seekers. Such deportations have included adults, families, and unaccompanied minors. On the US side of the USA–Mexico border, asylum seekers who had been detained before March 2020 have been given the option to either separate from their children or remain as family units. In the latter case, parents were forced to waive their children's right to parole. Waiving such a right implied having children in detention with their parents under carceral conditions for longer than twenty days.

Separations, however, have also been politically motivated. In the United States, following an open anti-migration political platform and adding to pre-existing stereotypes that further criminalized undocumented migrants, from April 2018 until June 2018, the Trump administration put into effect a 'zero-tolerance policy'. This policy allowed for the separation of children—as young as eight months of age—from their parents or caregivers (Morrison, Fredericks & Agrawal 2018: 2). Minors, who for the most part could not communicate in the dominant language, were placed in overcrowded holding facilities with little to no explanation on their condition, the length of their detentions, or their caregivers' whereabouts. With no initial intent to eventually unify children with their parents, the governments' harsh measures were meant to act, according to Donald Trump, as a deterrent. It was assumed that persecuting adults for illegal crossings and separating them from their children would eventually lower the numbers of undocumented individuals infiltrating the US–Mexican border (Amezcua 2019: 37, 50, 54, 68).

CHILD AND ADOLESCENT MIGRATION, MENTAL HEALTH, AND LANGUAGE

Push factors and immigration policies are in a constant state of change. This has been seen in the USA prior to and following its most recent change in administration. Presently, even though the closure of the US border remains in place, Biden's administration has brought into relief a more humanitarian approach to unaccompanied entries. While still discouraging illegal crossings, Biden has reduced the number of unaccompanied children denied entry to the USA (BBC 2022: para. 6). As a consequence, many parents and caregivers who had been waiting with their children on the Mexican side of the border have been making the unimaginable decision to pay smugglers to help their children to make the perilous journey across the border as unaccompanied minors.

Human Trafficking and Its Impact on Separations

In 'Detention of migrant children', Linton, Griffin, and Shapiro (2017) describe the difference in immigration pathways between accompanied and unaccompanied children. Linton et. al argue that the conspicuous problem of human trafficking influences the protocol that is followed for accompanied children. In the United States, there is a high incidence of trafficked children coming from Mexico and Canada. Hence, as mentioned above, if undocumented travellers are apprehended, and if such travellers cross the American border with one or more children, immigration officials attempt to verify the biological relationship. If a biological relationship is not established, children are separated from adults and considered unaccompanied minors (2).

As with adults, not all children are allowed access to their intended destination. The treatment children receive while detained by immigration officials depends on whether they are accompanied or unaccompanied. If a child travels with a family unit, their entry depends on their qualification for asylum.[10] When minors travel alone, protocols vary depending on their identity verification, officials' ability to connect with family members residing in the child's home country or the country of transit. Officials also look at minors' possible ties to criminal activities, including human trafficking and exploitation.

As seen in the United States, attitudes towards immigration change over time. Trump's government was led by anti-immigration rhetoric. Such rhetoric, as we have explored above, has been challenged by Biden. Recently, a shift towards more humanitarian approaches to migration may be taking place in the United States. Yet, again, as highlighted by Amnesty International, the

36

United States should continue to improve its practices. While many minors and their families are exempted from deportation, children coming from Mexico are still repatriated BBC 2022: para. 6).

Furthermore, amid important changes enacted by the new US administration, some of Biden's predecessor's anti-immigration policies are still in place. In an apparent effort to prevent the spread of Covid in holding facilities, Biden announced that Title 42 will remain in place, at least until our global health crisis and 'the spread of non-citizens stops being a "serious danger" to public health' (para. 8). Title 42 is a policy instated during the Trump administration. As noted by BBC News, this immigration policy 'allows for US authorities to automatically expel almost all undocumented migrants seeking entry, bypassing normal immigration laws and protections' (BBC 2022: para. 5).

Here it seems rational to suggest that with the increase in illegal entries since the start of Biden's current term, and the danger posed by Covid, regardless of the current administration's claimed humanitarian approach to immigration, Biden may follow, at least in part, the steps taken by his predecessor(s).

Children in US Processing and Customs Enforcement Residential Centres

Following apprehension in the United States, accompanied and unaccompanied minors are held by the Department of Homeland Security in Customs and Border Protection Processing centres for brief periods. This preliminary detention takes place before 1) repatriation, 2) release into the community, either as family units or with community sponsors while awaiting immigration hearings, or 3) being transferred to non-secure facilities. Accompanied and unaccompanied children are normally detained in processing centres for five to seven days. Yet during the increased influx of minors, preliminary detentions could be extended to twenty days. After such time, if adults continue to be detained, children are either 1) separated, as described previously, or 2) transferred, alone or with their families, to shelters or Custom Enforcement Residential Centres.[11] Although such protocols are followed for some children and family units, many remain in processing centres or are moved to secured holding centres for indeterminate periods. Regardless of their length of stay, the United States' processing and family residential centres operate below national and international standards. Even when housed for a brief period, detainment

CHILD AND ADOLESCENT MIGRATION, MENTAL HEALTH, AND LANGUAGE

in carceral environments with limited services and little to no information on legal protocols and potential release has an inevitable effect on minors' vulnerable condition and mental health.

Processing centres are locked enclosures that vary in size. Detainees often sleep on cement floors. They have open toilets, no bathing facilities, constant light exposure, and insufficient food and water. In such centres individuals are also denied access to medical care and have their belongings, including phones and medications, confiscated for the length of their stay. The lack of information and the separation from loved ones are other salient markers of stress incurred in these facilities. Children and families have limited or no comprehensive orientation about the immigration process. They do not know their detention length. Often, they have no access to legal counsel (Linton, Griffin & Shapiro 2017: 4–5). Adults are commonly separated by gender. When accompanied, children under the age of eighteen stay with their mothers. Separation occurs when a child is detained with their father. In such a case, the adult male is moved to a male holding area, while the child, as is the case with unaccompanied children, is housed in a female holding area (Linton, Griffin & Shapiro 2017: 5; Kronick, Rousseau & Cleveland 2018: 424).

In the event of moving from processing centres to holding centres, in addition to the lack of provided information and the possible continuation of separations, children and families are provided limited and delayed physical and mental health services, as well as inadequate education services (Linton, Griffin & Shapiro 2017: 5). Family residential centres for accompanied children are described as places in which multiple families stay in dormitory-style rooms. Such rooms are generally for mothers and children. However, a discrepancy can be observed between stipulated standards and the care and conditions offered to minors and their families at these centres. Even though the Flores Settlement Agreement stipulates that children should be held in the least restricted environment, these centres are enclosed prison-like facilities with limited dental, medical, and mental health services (5).

While a small number of unaccompanied children are placed in foster care, unaccompanied minors who are not repatriated or released to the community under the care of relatives or sponsors are held in different types of facilities that range in size and level of security. In such facilities, children are provided 'dormitory-style rooms, shared bathrooms, showers, clothes, hot meals, year-round educational services, recreational activities, and limited legal services'

MIGRATION AND TRAUMA

(Linton, Griffin & Shapiro 2017: 5). Added to this is the grim reality that unaccompanied minors' and families' conditions in the United States have deteriorated further since the cited 2017 publication. In 2018, even though the Flores Settlement Agreement remained and continues to remain in effect in the United States to this date (Schweikart 2019: 1), the mental strains imposed on children and families by immigration practices were heightened between April and June, as explained in the following section.

A Continued Examination of Detention Centres

Many publications and newspaper articles across Canada, across the United States, and abroad have openly criticized American immigration measures, emphasizing that separations violate international laws while negatively affecting children's mental health. In 'Separated and sick: an immigrant child's traumatic experience of illness and recovery', Morrison, Fredricks and Agrawal (2018) describe the horrifying experiences of a nine-year-old child from Honduras. After being isolated from her father and detained in an over-crowded shelter, this child developed aseptic meningitis and type A influenza (2). Following her high fever and seizures, she was taken to a hospital where she was treated in an intensive care unit. As described in this article, in time, even though her critical condition eventually improved, her 'mental state was severely compromised' (2). Aside from describing her condition and the lack of approval for psychological services at the hospital, Morrison et al. highlight:

> Public Health research has revealed that adverse childhood events have seri-
> ous negative effects on children's development and long-term physical and
> emotional health. Children who experience an adverse childhood event have
> a much higher long-term risk of depression, suicidality, and substance abuse,
> among other medical conditions. (Morrison, Fredricks & Agrawal 2018: 2)

In line with other publications, the article also quotes the American Academy of Pediatrics' comments on minors' condition as detainees:

> Young detainees may experience developmental delay and poor psychological
> adjustment, potentially affecting functioning in school. Qualitative reports
> about detained ... immigrant children in the United States found high rates
> of posttraumatic stress disorder, anxiety, depression, suicidal ideation, and
> other behavioural problems. Additionally, expert consensus concluded that

39

even brief detention could cause psychological trauma and induce long-term mental health risks for children. (Cited in Morrison, Fredricks & Agrawal 2018: 2)

Unfortunately, the physical and psychological problems associated with children's and adolescents' immigration detentions and the lack of available services are not limited to the United States. Canada, a country known for taking pride in its pluricultural make-up, linguistic diversity, and history as the first country to establish a Multicultural Policy (Dewing 2013: 3), continues to detain children in immigration holding centres. Regardless of its international image as a humanitarian country built by migrants, Canada continues to detain individuals and families in detention centres next to or within its international airports.

The complexity of this problem is worth highlighting. Despite international pressures to increase immigration quotas and research demonstrating the negative consequences of detention, Canadian holding centres continue to operate beyond capacity.[12]

Canada's Approach to Unlawful Entries and Immigration Detentions

As reported by the Global Detention Project (GDP),[13] even though Canada's current prime minister has begun a reform to change Canada's immigration and detention practices (2018: 3), concerns regarding Canada's receiving protocols remain. These include Canada's detention of children, and other vulnerable individuals,[14] in carceral environments for undetermined lengths of detention,[15] offering limited alternatives to holding centres for families, overreliance on maximum-security prisons for detainees,[16] and the absence of an institutionalized framework for complaints (14). Equally important is the secrecy and lack of transparency on behalf of the Canadian government (20). Canada's general population has limited knowledge of detention locations, detainees' treatment, and the insufficiency of viable health, mental, legal, and educational services for all detainees, including children.

Canada's existing Immigration and Refugee Protection Act (IRPA), which provides the grounds for detaining all foreign nationals, including children, controls and regulates detentions and determines conditions of release.[17] This Act was framed shortly after the 9/11 terrorist attacks on US soil (4). Thus, in Canada, when immigration laws are violated, immigration policies and the measures taken are austere. With illegal entries and/or unauthorized stays, the use of detention or holding centres is common. The grounds for detention of permanent residents and foreign nationals[18] include immigration officials' need to verify identity, prove that a foreign national is not a danger to the nation or persons, confirm that such an individual is not considered a flight risk while proceedings take place,[19] and attest that the immigrant is not part of a group of irregular entrants that may be involved with human trafficking and exploitation (5–6, 8).

The IRPA affords officials broad powers to detain, incarcerate, and deport individuals 'based on mere suspicions or secret evidence' (4). Immigration detentions may occur without warrants, and asylum seekers may be detained during or throughout their proceedings. In addition, even if criminal charges have not been raised, if an individual has been issued a 'security certificate' and is thus suspected to be a threat to national security or a danger to any person, they may be detained for long periods—years—without a hearing (7).

Minors and Immigration Detentions in Canada

As mentioned throughout this chapter, while international laws have been in place to protect children's best interests (Kronick, Rousseau, and Cleveland 2018: 423), accompanied and unaccompanied minors are apprehended in Canada. Minors and adults are detained for various lengths of time. These range from a few days to well over a year (Global Detention Project 2018: 12; Kronick, Rousseau & Cleveland 2018: 423–24). As stated in the Immigration, Refugees and Citizenship Canada (IRCC) Enforcement Manual, the Canada Border Services Agency (CBSA) implements a framework intended to keep children out of detentions and keep families together 'as much as humanly possible'. Accordingly, unless family units are expatriated or children are released to the community, children are commonly housed with their detained parent(s) (Global Detention Project 2018: 3, 9).

As mentioned earlier, other reasons for children's detainment include being considered a flight risk or needing to have their identity confirmed (9). Canadian detentions or holding centres are secured buildings with limited resources.[20] As in the United States, in these carceral environments, those detained are commonly segregated by gender. Children are generally housed in female areas. Less often, children are separated from their parents and placed in foster care (9–10).

CHILD AND ADOLESCENT MIGRATION, MENTAL HEALTH, AND LANGUAGE

Those who work with migrant communities understand the short- and long-term negative effects of child incarcerations. In a publication titled 'Refugee children's sandplay narratives in immigration detention in Canada', researchers Rachel Kronick, Cécile Rousseau, and Janet Cleveland (2018) report the results of their examination of the realities affecting detained children aged three to thirteen. Their findings, drawn from a triangulation of interviews, participant observation, and elicitations from children's real and imagined stories, pointed to a deterioration in children's mental health. As they claim, the human violence and terror that some may have experienced before their incarceration, along with their difficult migration process, confinement, surveillance, and precarious status, amounts to the expression of minors' hopelessness and depression (425, 430–31, 433).

Children's and adolescents' subjective experiences are informed by the ambivalence that stems from feeling unprotected by their legal guardians and the Canadian authorities. Children who have been separated from their loved ones while in detention feel abandoned. Regardless of agency and willingness to relocate, unaccompanied minors also feel alone and unprotected. Adding to the problem, even though medical services are provided to those detained, minors are not granted access to education. In addition, unless they are housed with siblings, minors are not granted means for socialization or exposure to fellow children of their same age group (434). Young migrants' descriptions of their detentions highlight their sense of isolation, vulnerability, and ability to conceptualize their past and present realities. Aligned with their hopelessness and distress, children's stories pointed to their lack of vision for the foreseeable future (429). The feeling of being stuck in a never-ending present, with an unattainable past and an unforeseeable future, is by definition a sign of trauma (Carra-Salsberg 2017: 26).

Conclusion

This chapter drew attention to the conditions affecting minors when in transit or when trying to become established in host countries. With a focus on irregular entries, it examined child–parent and child–sponsor separations, as well as conditions at government-run and makeshift refugee camps. This chapter also looked at individual and family detentions, highlighting the conditions and the limited services offered at holding centres. It drew attention to children's

MIGRATION AND TRAUMA

invisibility at such centres and the implications of systemic neglect. While examining circumstances affecting makeshift and government-run refugee camps and hotspots, this second chapter stressed the prevalence of symbolic, systemic, and physical violence. It highlighted the problems associated with camps' poor sanitary conditions and food shortages. Equally importantly, this chapter reviewed how in the case of most receiving systems, children's rights are often violated regardless of the laws established to ensure their best interests.

Building on Akhtar's (2012) conception of our human, universal needs, we understand that experiencing a sense of physical and emotional safety and compassion for one's past and present realities is of utmost importance to our well-being. This assertion applies to individuals of all ages and walks of life, yet it is especially true for children. Keeping such a concept at the forefront of our discussion is essential when thinking about international migrations. As argued throughout this chapter, for accompanied and unaccompanied minors, their crises result from the amalgamation of adverse pre- and post-migration occurrences, as well as stressors that may affect them while in transit. Following their relocation and if they are allowed to remain—permanently or temporarily—within the host country, stressors may also stem from their sociopolitical and affective condition as newcomers and as linguistic, ethnocultural, and racial minorities.

This chapter's study of the dynamics influencing migrants' contested journeys aimed at better lives is intended to provide readers with a foundation for a better understanding of the ensuing chapters' examination of newcomers' socio-affective experiences of acculturation. By defining impersonal and/or intersubjective and intra-psychic traumas and applying socio-psychological, semiotic, and psychoanalytic theories of language acquisition and socialization, the upcoming chapters continue to study the interconnected and developmental realities that directly and indirectly affect child and adolescent migrants.

3 Memory within Language: Our Mother Tongue's Link to Subjective Development and our Remembered and Seemingly Forgotten Sense of Being, Loving, and Belonging

[H]istory, like trauma, is never simply one's own ... history is precisely the way we are implicated in each other's traumas.

(Caruth 1996: 24)

An Integrated View of Young Migrants' Experiences within Languages

With a focus on the developmental significance of language, let us now consider how, while our cry as infants signalled our need to have our most basic demands met, our primary language, once learned, internalized, and articulated, opened the doors to exchanges and meanings that exceeded our basic needs for physical survival. At the conscious level, our language is the vehicle that establishes our link to the external world. It grants us our universal desire to connect with others, remember and articulate our past, understand our present, and project a future. Through this phenomenon and its relation to our known and seemingly forgotten memories, we experience a sense of continuity across time. As argued in this book's first chapter, our symbolic code of meanings plays a significant role in our ongoing conceptualizations, social interactions, and sense of self in relation to others. It is the essence through which we voice our socio-emotional concerns, and display or attempt to hide our affections, our past and present fears, and hopes. At the unconscious level,

MEMORY WITHIN LANGUAGE

our symbolic code of meanings becomes key to our emotional and psycho-sexual development. It is a vehicle that marks, while becoming marked by, our unconscious drives and defences. It is a human singularity that carries the emotional weight of our remembered and seemingly forgotten beginnings (Carra-Salsberg 2017: 12, 25).

Taking an integrated approach to our study of language's psycho-emotional and social meanings is key when conceptualizing the condition of migrants. It is central to the study of the emotions that child and adolescent newcomers often experience when learning, and later internalizing, a second language. This chapter takes a psychoanalytic approach to the study of a primary language's relation to children's and adolescents' socio-emotional and sexual development. It begins with psychoanalytic theories that pay close attention to individuals' stages of psychosexual and socio-affective growth, and studies their relation to the concurrent development of a primary language. It examines how language becomes intimately linked to subjects' history of affect, pre-linguistic trauma, and identifications.

Language as a Remnant

For much of her life, Hannah Arendt engaged in work that was meaningful to her healing process. When looking at her history, we learn that in Germany, during the years leading to World War II, she responded to the growing oppression taking place in her country by agreeing to collect proof of anti-Semitic propaganda. Her actions, which were meant to expose and even hinder the dominant party, led to her arrest and interrogation at the hands of the Gestapo. Following her release, the threat of persecution led to her escape from Germany to France, and eventually, to the United States. Arendt's need to contest and intellectualize the force behind Nazism continued beyond her initial and later relocations. While in France, she helped resettle Jewish children in present-day Israel. Following her move to the United States, Arendt became (re-)immersed within the world of academia and invested the remaining part of her career in politics, history, and the understanding of our human condition. Years following the culmination of World War II, in a 1964 interview with Günter Gaus, Arendt was asked to reminisce on an aspect of pre-war Germany that had been left unchanged. Her brief, ambiguous response has led to many theoretical discussions to this date: 'What remains? The language remains' (Baehr 2000: 12).

45

CHILD AND ADOLESCENT MIGRATION, MENTAL HEALTH, AND LANGUAGE

Building upon the arguments of the previous chapter, we may assume that for Arendt, what had remained was language's ability to bestow upon its users a subject position—one that grants individuals the capacity to share, reason, and conceptualize the overlapping realities that form part of their intricate worlds. In a similar vein, in *Remnants of Auschwitz*, Giorgio Agamben (1999) suggests that Arendt's answer points to how language endures the history of its speakers. Agamben highlights how language and testimony survive the people who speak them. Language, he claims, is a field traversed by two opposing tensions: 1) anomia, which is the movement towards innovation and transformation, and 2) the norm, which moves towards stability and preservation. The speaking subject, who decides what is sayable from unsayable, is at the intersection of these tensions. A speaker's decision to share or omit, continues Agamben, becomes defined and transmitted through their speech and resulting testimony (158–60). For Agamben, what remains following Auschwitz is the act of bearing witness: survivors sharing the seemingly impossible truth in place of those who could no longer testify (145–51). Along such lines, Theodor Adorno argues that since thought could not be reconciled with experience, Auschwitz involves the aporic act of representing the unrepresentable (cited in Luckhurst 2008: 5). While considering Agamben's and Adorno's arguments, we may suggest that for Arendt, what remains lies within language's influential scope of representing and bearing witness to an unrepresentable truth—one that propelled Arendt's need to understand the inconceivable actions that affected her life and search for reason.

From a different angle, in a conference titled *The Future of Testimony*, Shoshana Felman (2011) linked Arendt's response to the fact that, despite her own migrations and the challenges she encountered in Germany, while in the United States and within the private realm, Arendt continued to interact primarily in her mother tongue. By paying close attention to Arendt's interview with Gaus, we note that Felman's argument is validated in the manner in which Arendt expresses her emotional connection to the German language. During a post-war visit, when hearing German freely spoken on the streets, Arendt described feeling a "violent emotion" of 'indescribable joy' (Baehr 2000: 14). Here we may add that regardless of the negative events that marked her past experiences, the post-war return to her home country and her re-immersion into her German tongue reawakened her seemingly dormant emotional ties to her primary language. Founded on Sigmund Freud's (1930, 2002) description of our history of affect in *Civilization and its Discontents* (10), one may propose that Arendt's visit brought to light the 'oceanic feelings' she experienced while becoming enveloped by the flow and sounds of her mother tongue. Within this context, we may also suggest that Arendt's response may also be linked to Lacan's (1974–75) 'Imaginary' register, 'jouissance', and the pre-linguistic experience of '*lalangue*'.

In *Civilization and Its Discontents*, Freud argues that the oceanic feeling is a perception of 'a feeling of something limitless, unbounded ... a purely subjective fact ... a feeling ... of being indissolubly bound up with and belonging to a world outside of oneself' (2002: 3–4). This experience is one Freud annexed to religion and to subjects' universal need to belong, to feel protected and loved. Central to our discussion, the oceanic feeling reflects an infant's experience of being swaddled, sheltered, and protected by their first love(s). This feeling and impression may also be connected to Lacan's discussion of the imaginary stage of development and infants' pre-linguistic jouissance. For infants, this pre-linguistic affective experience stems from the joy they encounter through their incoherent articulations. Through the law of relationality, it is commonsensical to extend Lacan's jouissance to the tandem experience of hearing the sounds of one's primary language (Gutiérrez-Peláez 2015: 139–41).

By leaning on the arguments offered by Freud and Lacan, we may suggest that for Arendt, her mother tongue may have brought to light the remnants of her infantile history: her remembered and seemingly forgotten memories of being loved, protected, and nurtured as an infant, a child and later, an adolescent. Despite Arendt's remembered history of oppression within extended sociopolitical circles in Germany, her primary language may have been the phenomenon that brought back the joy and reassurance she experienced at home. Along such lines and also in her 1964 interview, Arendt shared how her home had always been a place of safety. She described it as a holding environment that offered her a respite from the politics and everyday discrimination that she, as a child, witnessed at school (Baehr 2000: viii). Even though Arendt spent most of her life away from the socio-geographical and cultural space that encompassed her native land, Germany remained as a continuum that held together her lifelong experiences. Here we may assume that regardless of the war that swept across Europe, regardless of her need to flee from Germany and escape from the anti-Semitic threat that affected her life, German, Arendt's primary language, continued to exist as a vibrant part of her master affect.

CHILD AND ADOLESCENT MIGRATION, MENTAL HEALTH, AND LANGUAGE

Our Conscious and Unconscious Interactions within and through Language

A psychoanalytic lens allows for an insight into the complexity of language. To paraphrase Salman Akhtar (2012), all forms of mentation, resulting perceptions, and behaviours derive from an admixture of primary and secondary processes (n.p.). As split subjects, we are affected by known and seemingly forgotten histories that stem from interactions with the social and with our earlier and later selves. This argument may be best conceptualized through Deborah Britzman's (2006) explanation of our third space. In *Novel Education*, Britzman argues that all self–other dynamics occur within an area of experiencing governed by an unconscious 'give and take': where we unknowingly respond to others' psychic histories and resulting affect as much as others respond to our own histories of affect (42–44, 49). This cultural space, as also addressed by Winnicott (2005), is a terrain of perceptions and interactions that mark the development of our personalities. Such a terrain is one of ongoing socio-affective growth, as well as our dynamic sense of being and existing.

This idea of becoming influenced by an exponential chain of repetitions, interpretations, and introjections was central to Chapter 1's discussion of language. It is also linked to this chapter's examination of Arendt's 1964 interview and the condition that affects young, formerly monolingual migrants. Arendt, in her discussion with Gaus, stated that 'we can never become fully aware of all the forces that influence us ... nor can we ever know what comes of our actions' Baehr 2000: 21). By highlighting our 'unawareness' of the multiplicity of voices and experiences that shape us, Arendt touches upon the known and unknown dynamics that exist within language. Even though Arendt's discourse has been tied to speakers' conscious realm, acknowledging, once again, that our everyday actions and perceptions are shaped by an admixture of primary and secondary processes, Arendt knowingly and unknowingly situates her argument within the realm of language, psychoanalysis, and our realities as split subjects.

Children's Universal Development within Language, Otherness, and Trauma

To best conceptualize a language's intrinsic significance, let us take a psychoanalytic approach to the study of children's psychosexual development. Jacques

MEMORY WITHIN LANGUAGE

Lacan's (1969–70) interpretation of Freud's Oedipus Complex argues that an infant's subjectivity lies in their positioning within and understanding of their immediate social cell (Felman 1987: 104).[1] He suggests that a child's development occurs within a triangulated structure that involves the infant, the maternal figure, and the paternal figure.[2] During the initial stage of postnatal life, the mother figure or primary caregiver becomes the child's first love object. Before the child acknowledges their father's presence, the child's primary caregiver encompasses the infant's entire world. As such, child–mother boundaries become blurred, and their identities are mirrored and merged as one (Eagleton 1983: 164; Felman 1989: 113). During the pre-Oedipal period, the child's symbiotic relation with the mother is an 'imaginary' one (Felman 1989: 113). At this stage, mothers or mothering symbols symbolize the child's first self-love. Since the child is unable to differentiate themselves from the mother, the child's love is narcissistic. Thus, it represents the child's love for their own body and self-image (104).[3]

What matters most to our discussion is that this 'Imaginary' register, as argued by Lacan, is one of ego identification, jouissance,[4] and the pre-linguistic experience of '*lalangue*'. When discussing Lacan's work, Gutiérrez-Peláez (2015) suggests that 'the child's *lalangue* is grounded in the physical/sensual experience of the infant engrossed in sensual production of sound, and the free expression of "itself" in the absence of the Other. The babbling or chirping is not addressed to the Other; it lies in a private experience that mobilizes a *jouissance*' (141). Unlike language's trans-individual nature, *lalangue* is a non-communicative, homophonic, private phenomenon. It is an experience that encompasses the child's earliest state of love and joy. This jouissance predates the anxiety that erupts through the child's later awareness of the 'Symbolic Order' (140–41), as well as the anxiety born from the subject's never-ending search for a unified self (Gallop 2012: 123).

At six months, before the Symbolic Order, the child develops an emerging concept of selfhood through the discovery of their reflection. During this period, known as the mirror stage, the child–mirror boundaries are merged, and the child becomes situated within a confounding paradox: the mirrored image becomes part of the child, while at the same time alien. In due course and while still within the Imaginary stage, the child forms an integrated self-image through their reflection. By then, this reflection offers them a gratifying image of a unified self. Through identifying with this mirrored image, the

49

child's sense of self is constructed by the 'I' reflected back by a person or an object in the world (Eagleton 1983: 164–65). This developmental experience initiates the individual's unremitting identifications with and link to the external world.

Following the establishment of the Imaginary stage and the child's developmental experience through their reflection, the child becomes aware of the father's presence. Such an encounter brings into awareness a world that exists beyond that of the mother's and the child's own. The father's presence, moreover, gives the child a pre-established structure. Within this 'Symbolic' register, the child's understanding of his social positioning occurs along with the development of language and communication. The Symbolic, suggests Lacan, involves the father, the law of incestual prohibition, and language: the first 'no' articulated through the linguistic system. As argued by Felman (1987), for Lacan 'desire and ability to symbolize' drive the child to use and situate themselves within language. This Lacanian theory stresses that speech occurs through, and is driven by, the infant's need in the form of desire: the child's desire to call, to address, to be addressed, and to be positioned within the Oedipus structure. Through such desire, the child is motivated to internalize and become an active part of our human discourse (113, 118).

To advance the previous chapter's discussion of language and subjects' internalization of pre-existing belief systems, we note that the child introjects societal rules within the Symbolic Order. These include sexual behaviours and thoughts that are either deemed acceptable or unacceptable. Concurrent with the development of language, this stage marks the incipience of the child's superego. With the father's appearance, and out of unconscious guilt, the child's incestual desire becomes repressed, and the self emerges as a split conscious–unconscious subject (Eagleton 1983: 165; Felman 1987: 113). As the child introjects the father's name (Felman 1987: 115), the earlier interpretation of the mother, as the sole representative of the child's love and external reality, is affected, and the imaginary bond established with the mother is relinquished. Consequently, the child becomes severed from his body, and as argued by Eagleton (1983), 'plunged into [the shock and trauma of] post-structural anxiety' (160).

Continuing with Lacan's work, let us stress that along with the Imaginary and Symbolic registers, the child becomes subjected to the realm of 'the Real'. This realm involves the encroachment of the Symbolic and Imaginary orders.

MEMORY WITHIN LANGUAGE

The Real, according to Gutiérrez-Peláez (2015), is not accessible to language or to phantasy, yet touches upon while haunting both (143–45). The unconscious trauma children experience characterizes this third order. This universal trauma, argues Gutiérrez-Peláez, is not reflected in the unsymbolized, violent, intense, unforeseeable experience. Instead, the unconscious trauma involving the Real arises when children enter the Symbolic Order. It is one that infests the infant's body and psyche through its erogenous zones. In agreement with Bion (1962a), Gutiérrez-Peláez asserts that, for the child, there is 'a nameless dread' as well as a 'dread of the name' (cited in Gutiérrez-Peláez 2015: 146). Even though it takes place within language, it does not appear in symbolic narration, or in the phantasies inherent to it. Instead, it is an experience that, according to Gutiérrez-Peláez, can never be verbalized (145).

Consistent with this view, when describing the traumatic dimensions of language, Gutiérrez-Peláez (2015) argues:

> Language is traumatic in various ways. Words can hurt, degrade, conjure, and produce anxiety. Words can be unforgettable; they determine destinies. Words can take hold of the body, mark it, and transform it, as hysterics have taught us. Language is also traumatic through the *lalangue* it carries, those non-communicative aspects of language, a private tongue, tongue mobilizing a form of *jouissance* that can produce an unpleasant satisfaction for it lays beyond the Freudian pleasure principle. Finally, language is traumatic because it definitively transforms an infant's relation to the world, leaving only subtle traces of what that relation prior to language could have been. (143)

Here we note how *lalangue* and language form part of speakers' history of affect. While *lalangue* envelops speakers' first narcissistic love, language is involved with early and later object relations. It propels while becoming marked by the child's introduction to societal behaviours and expectations, and their gradual transition into becoming a subject.

Our Primary Language's Link to our Remembered and Seemingly Forgotten Sense of Feeling, Loving, and Belonging

Language's developmental significance is also examined by D.W. Winnicott (2005) in his book *Playing and Reality*. His theory of personality and healthy development focuses on a child's transition from being as one with their primary caregiver to transitioning towards their independence. His theory draws attention to the importance of providing a child with a good enough environment to allow an intermediate area of experiencing and reality testing (2, 5). Through the actions of their mother, the young child transitions from the pleasure principle and initial sense of omnipotence to recognizing the reality principle and accepting their role within it (3). According to Winnicott, during the child's first six months, a 'good enough mother' is one that fully adapts to her infant's nourishing needs. This adaptation is essential for a child's initial development. It allows for the child to construct an illusion of omnipotence by believing that the mother is a part of an external reality that corresponds to their capacity to create (14–16). At six months of age, the mother's task is to wean the infant by a natural process of gradual disillusionment.[5] Through weaning, the child can eventually tolerate frustration, understand that objects are real and not an illusion, and be both hated and loved. Correspondingly, the child perceives the reality that exists outside the self (14–15).

A child's transition, continues Winnicott, from the magical to the real, occurs between the ages of six and twelve months. During this phase, the child becomes attached to an external object. This object is a tangible article that is perceived as a defence against anxiety. It helps the infant adapt to independence from their mother (5). This object, known as the transitional object, reflects the continuity of the child's experience (5). It is never considered by the child as part of their body, yet it is not fully recognized by the infant as part of the external world (2–3). As highlighted by Winnicott, a transitional object is the original 'not me' possession that exists within the subjective and what is objectively perceived (4–6, 12). Winnicott explains that the object's symbolism and significance rests in the way in which it stands for the breast or mother (8). This transitional object is perceived as more important than the mother, and thus it becomes an almost inseparable part of the infant's life (9).

This first observable possession that is 'never under magical control' (13) 'becomes an active part of the child's journey towards experiencing' (8). This object aids in positioning the infant within an introjected, subjective reality. It facilitates the infant's healthy transition into becoming a subject by promoting the development of their ego boundaries. It allows the child to accept, relate to, and form a conception of an external, shared reality (3, 14). The object

MEMORY WITHIN LANGUAGE

itself is not the transition. Instead, it represents and enables the transition from the feeling of being merged with the mother to a state of being in relation with the mother as something outside and separate (19–20). Winnicott argues that this object is not an internal mental object, or an external one (12–13). It is a possession that creates a neutral area of experience. It is part of a phenomenon that, once again, allows the infant to develop from the pleasure principle to the reality principle (13). Due to its intrinsic and developmental significance, explains Winnicott, the transitional phenomenon 'should not be challenged' (14, 17).

Winnicott's discussion of a subject's transition towards experiencing has much relevance to our epistemological discussion of language. Presented with previous notions on the subjective meaning and developmental function of a lived primary code, we can extend Winnicott's theory of the transitional phenomenon to our conceptualization of a primary language. We understand that a mother tongue represents the transition from being merged with the mother to being in relation with the mother as something outside and separate. A first tongue is a phenomenon that the child internalizes through its connection with their first object of affection. It is perceived as a part of the subject and thus a possession that eventually forms our intermediate area of experiencing. For the child, the mother tongue is separate from them as a speaking subject, while it is not entirely part of their external reality. For a child, a mother tongue exists between what is subjectively perceived and objectively observed. Interconnected with our discussion of Lacan and the mirror stage, a primary language is the medium, like the mirror, through which the subject receives a response to their address. It is tied to their earliest stage of life and is the key to the child's development, introjections, and sense of self. It embodies while forming part of the area between the individual's inner and shared realities, forming a significant part of a subject's third space and the interchangeable authority that such space holds.

The connection between our primary language, the unconscious, and our ego development is not limited to Freud's and Lacan's work. A primary language, which, in agreement with Salman Akhtar (2012: n.p.), is the closest to a child's maternal imago, has the dichotomized effect of becoming linked with the mother while aiding in the child's first individuation and inevitable pull away from her. In *The Beast in the Nursery*, Adam Phillips (1998) links a mother tongue to the child's introduction to the greater community of competent speakers. He looks at how a primary language is also involved in the child's renunciation of the perception of their mother's undivided love and attention (43). Likewise, Alice Pitt (2013) highlights that a mother tongue is part of a loss associated with the child's realization that for the mother, there is a world of objects and desires that exists separate from the child (41). Such recognition, claim both Phillips and Pitt, marks the inevitable transition that gives way to the child's development as a subject: as one who is paradoxically linked and yet separate from their first object (Phillips 1998: 43–45; Pitt 2013: 41).

Language and Identification

The attention to a primary language's involvement in children's psycho-emotional and social development is of much relevance to this book's focus on child and adolescent migration and mental health. Such attention sheds light onto how, for migrant children and youth, introjecting and identifying with the host reality shapes the child's conscious and unconscious development and relation to their mother or primary caregiver. In the *Encyclopedia of Personality and Individual Differences*, Laura Cariola (2017) divides introjections into individuals' primary and secondary unconscious responses to the external environment. While both are assumed to be part of normative development, primary identifications 'relate to early infancy when the self is not differentiated from external objects'. Secondary identifications, on the other hand, become a mode of psychological development that continues throughout the individual's life cycle (n.p.). Through the latter, the subject introjects external objects in order to 'build mental representations and schemas of the self and the external world' (n.p.). By quoting Piaget (1954), Cariola points to how these include various cognitive modes: 'sensorimotor, lexical and symbolic' (n.p.). With secondary identifications, unlike primary infantile identifications, the subjects differentiate themselves from external objects.

Deborah Britzman (2006) describes secondary identifications as a defence mechanism, involving the ego's unconscious response to the perceptual threat of the environment (44). Through this mechanism, the ego aims at 'reducing feelings of separation and hostility and increasing feelings of closeness between the self and the external object' (Freud 1923/2001b; Cariola 2017: n.p.). This defence, continues Britzman, which is founded on ego psychology and object relation theory, takes place at the higher developmental level (44). Secondary identifications are a twofold unconscious response: they allow the ego to fulfil the phantasy of taking in, or introjecting, aspects of its surrounding world into the self, to then project parts of itself—good and bad—into the Other (44). Through this process, the ego establishes a relation with the surrounding environment: it incorporates surrounding behaviours, attitudes, and ideologies and projects them back. These influence the subject's interpretation of their reality and responses to and from the Other.

Within our third space, identifications give rise to our sense of self and a fluid understanding of our social—and inner—worlds. Through ongoing, day-to-day introjections and projections our subjectivity is formed, informed, altered, and re-formed. Even though identifications take place throughout our lives, during their foundational years and early stages of ego development, children are more easily shaped through the identifications that become introjected through their surrounding environments. By means of such identifications, behaviours, ideologies, and ways of life become defined and redefined as their own. While these identifications are natural parts of children's and adolescents' personal growth, the problem for young migrants is encountered when the host country's behaviours and belief systems differ greatly from those of their caregivers. In such cases, the disparity between older and newer introjections, and the clash between caregivers' expectations and young migrants' need to individuate and assimilate, often adds to their disorientation, anxiety, guilt, and cumulative crisis.

Language and Individuations

A primary language supports speakers' cognitive growth and affective development. This phenomenon forms part of the establishment of the child–mother bond, while also aiding the child's transition away from the parent and towards the greater community of speakers. It plays a key role in children's and adolescents' individuations. As suggested by Akhtar (1995), the first separation-individuation phase, which occurs during childhood, is the first stepping stone for a child's identity formation (1052). The second separation-individuation stage takes place during adolescence and involves the subject's superego formation. This latter individuation, as argued by Winnicott (1986), is one of puberty changes, confusion, immaturity, shifts in ideals, and personal

CHILD AND ADOLESCENT MIGRATION, MENTAL HEALTH, AND LANGUAGE

disillusionment about the world of adults (24–25). Such disillusionment marks a degree of further separation from parents. When discussing individuals' healthy move towards independence, Winnicott claims that separation from family should never be complete. Being fully withdrawn from their family or nuclear cell leads to vulnerability. Accordingly, there should always be a degree of 'dependence on mental nurse or family' (21).

For child and adolescent migrants, the separation-individuation phases tend to be profound—and this provides the focus of this volume. Young migrants' move away from their nuclear cell is more significant when compared to that of non-migrants. This is especially true when there is a marked difference between parents' language and belief systems and those of the host communities surrounding their children. As argued by Akhtar (2012), the vaster the cultural clash, the greater the children's rebelliousness and sense of separation (n.p.). Drawing attention to children's developmental need to separate while still maintaining a degree of dependence on their family for emotional support is important for us to consider when studying unaccompanied minors' experiences. This is particularly relevant when minors physically separate from their parents, who are either deceased or, for the most part, unavailable to aid their children through their life transitions.

For accompanied children, the challenge undergone by their parents or caregivers is worth noting, especially because of the way such a challenge affects the dynamics that take place within their nuclear cell. This struggle is captured by Kathleen Saint-Onge (2013) in her autobiographical book *Bilingual Being*, when she notes: 'If monolingual, long-settled parents think their adolescents are slipping away from them, they should try spending a day in an immigrant's shoes' (47). As argued thus far, for many migrant parents, their children's natural process of individuation becomes heightened through the realization that on top of a normal generational gap, a shift in ideas and behaviours creates a greater gap— caused by having their children influenced by a culture and language parents may not fully understand or accept.

This clash in beliefs and, by extension, the conflicts that arise from parents' expectations is also highlighted by Aarti Shahani (2019) in her memoir when she recalls:

On Saturday nights, while my classmates were out living their lives— at concerts, on dates, building their 'extracurricular' bona fides at a city

MEMORY WITHIN LANGUAGE

shelter—I was stuck at the Shahani compound. It was Dad's time to feel
he still had the world he'd left behind, the one where your family is your
primary social life. (71)

In this brief quote Shahani draws attention to the difference in parental expectations and behaviours. While such difference is highlighted throughout her book, it is most apparent when she says:

It used to be Dad that was my biggest problem—the impregnable wall
between me and freedom, the dating and dancing police, the enforcer of skirt
lengths ... Dad absolutely treated girls and boys differently. He expected me
to be in the kitchen. (131)

First-generation adult migrants tend to idealize and ossify traditions that predate or are contemporaneous with their departure from their home country. While living in a host country, even though caregivers' ideas of acceptable and unacceptable behaviours—and gender-specific society roles—may change over time, many migrant parents maintain their past traditions and cultural expectations. Returning to Kathleen Saint-Onge's statement, parents who attempt to maintain past cultural beliefs struggle with the manner in which their children have naturally introjected host/dominant beliefs and how such introjection affects their children's overall behaviours.

As we have found, for children, the conflict that arises from their move away from their parents' traditions may result in parent–child confrontations and a sense of guilt. The latter is often heightened when the experience undergone by young migrants is compounded with the acquisition and internalization of the host language. Along such lines, in much of her memoir, Saint-Onge articulates this universal guilt that stems from replacing one's mother tongue: 'show me a bilingual person's autobiography and I'll show you someone who is apologizing for something' (xvii). This poorly understood guilt, which is commonly carried by migrant children and youth, is, once again, not only linked to shifts in perspectives, ideologies, and ways of life. It is intensified by the acquisition of a host language, and hence the child's inevitable move away from the language linked to their first loves. Children's and adolescents' separation-individuation may be increased by the anger that often stems from their parents' decision to migrate, and, possibly, the added strain that stems from the stigma attached to their condition as migrants.

CHILD AND ADOLESCENT MIGRATION, MENTAL HEALTH, AND LANGUAGE

Language Acquisition and Its Impact on Migrants' Translating Realities

As a language learner, educator, and a first-generation migrant, I understand that becoming immersed within the compounds of a foreign-host reality is, without a doubt, an anxiety-evoking occurrence. It is an experience that often evokes a sense of social and inner chaos. To continue our focus on childhood and adolescence, since most young migrants are enrolled in the host country's school system, socializing in the host language with teachers, school administrators, and peers becomes an inevitable occurrence. Their initial response to their newly imposed reality is founded on several factors. As discussed in this book's previous chapters, factors that give way to their anxiety and initial sense of displacement and/or marginalization may include—yet are not limited to—the similarity between migrants' culture and that of the host community, along with the dominant community's dialogical response to its newest members. For young, monolingual migrants, the problem of communication adds to the strain of becoming immersed within a reality that confuses and renders them foreign. The initial stages of linguistic and cultural immersion and host-language acquisition become a challenge. This is especially felt when students attempt to interact with those who form part of their new environment. An added challenge is felt through the personal estrangement that comes from the suddenness of their newly imposed identity. Such estrangement often leads to young learners' initial rejection of the host language and the overall reality it represents.

Focusing now on host-language acquisition, the relative ease with which newcomers are able to learn the new symbolic code varies with age and phase of psychic structuring. In addition to myelinization,[6] the ease or difficulty associated with language acquisition is tied to learners' ego development. Since speech and language are accomplishments of the ego (Stengel 1939: 475), the younger and less established individuals' ego boundaries are, the greater their ability to take in and become transformed through language (Akhtar 2012: n.p.). Along such lines, Guiora, Brannon, and Dull (1972) claim that when the ego's boundaries are not fixed, the ego is more permeable and, therefore, more willing to take on a new identity (cited in Block 2007: 51). This emphasis on ego development is also stressed by Douglas

58

MEMORY WITHIN LANGUAGE

Brown (1980) when, studying the highly transformative effects of language acquisition, he suggests:

> For any monolingual person the language ego involves the interaction of the native language and ego development. Your self-identity is inextricably bound up with your language, for it is in the communicative process—the process of sending out messages and having them 'bounce back'—that such identities are confirmed, shaped and reshaped. (Cited in Block 2007: 51–52)

By language ego, Douglas Brown means the learner's language-related identity and the changes it undergoes while acquiring a new language. This assertion is founded on the post-ctural understanding of the fluidity of our identity formations. To a great extent, his claim is consistent with Winnicott's (2005) theory of the development of an organized personality—specifically, in the manner in which the self is postulated through dynamic interactions with the Other and in how a personality develops by having their utterances reflected back (82–83).

The emphasis on age and the ego's developmental stage is also central in David Block's (2007) *Second Language Identities*. When analysing Guiora's work, Block highlights that the ego loses its permeability with age. As argued by Block, since children have a weak language ego, they are easily influenced and are open to the language input they receive (52). By contrast, adolescents are 'caught in the whirlwind of physical and emotional changes as their personalities are being formed for adulthood'. During the period of adolescence, asserts Block, individuals become more inhibited, and 'their ego permeability wanes' (52). In light of this reality, in a much earlier publication, Erwin Stengel (1939) suggests that 'To give a child a second language, means to give [them] a second method of play. The impulse to communicate, [to reach outwards and take in the outside world] ... makes use of the new language with pleasure' (478).

According to Stengel, during the initial stage of host-language exposure, older children, adolescents, and adults are less open to change because of a fear of sounding comic in the new language (477).[7] We understand that an individual's superego develops during adolescence. Its incipience is founded on the introjection of its external world—specifically, on others' views and judgements of acceptable/unacceptable behaviours. At this stage, concern over being judged may inhibit the way the ego projects itself onto the world and therefore behaves. For newcomers, the development of the superego also affects their speech production. Language learners' fear of being judged relates not only to their inability to find proper words in the new language but also to understand idioms or construct sentences. Unfortunately, their concern also extends to their accent and fear of sounding comic.

Such fear is described in *How Dare the Sun Rise*, as Uwiringiyimana (2017) remarks:

> I knew a little more English this time around. I hoped things might go more smoothly … But no. Seventh grade started out even worse than sixth … There was a group of girls who would ask me random questions so they could make fun of the way I spoke when I replied. They would repeat the words I said, mocking my accent and laughing hysterically … I stopped answering their questions … I hated school. (149)

Even when individuals' utterances are intelligible, newcomers' variance in acoustic speech patterns points to difference or foreignness (Munro 2003: 38–39). Uwiringiyimana's (2017) experience as a host-language learner highlights the relation between language and, once again, Winnicott's (2005) psychoanalytic theory on the development of an organized personality. For her, the sensed foreignness in her speech and her lack of host-language proficiency contributed to the phenomenology of her psycho-emotional perceptions.

When discussing Lambert's early work on host-/second-language learners' experiences, Block notes that accents become markers of alliances to communities (2007: 50). Along these lines, in 'What's your background?', Philip Riley argues that 'a language is the most powerful symbol of group membership' (1991: 275). At times, when individuals are not proficient in a language or when their speech denotes a phonetic difference, their utterance grounds them socially. They become unwillingly placed outside the community's margins. Such positioning becomes significant grounds for communicatively produced hegemonic relations.[8] As seen with Uwiringiyimana, young migrants often become caught within a framework that grants native speakers a higher hierarchic position, while demoting the social place of those with lower language proficiencies.

The Emotionality of Significant Language Acquisition

An added factor that influences migrants' language acquisition relates to the emotional consequence of a primary language. The conceptualization of our first language's affective worth is key to an understanding of the guilt that

MEMORY WITHIN LANGUAGE

surges from its replacement. As argued in my previous publications, when a second language becomes internalized, and a first language is no longer subservient to all primary and secondary processes, language learners often experience the poorly understood affective void that stems from the act of distancing ourselves from our first loves. Such a feeling is brilliantly highlighted by Alice Pitt (2013), who, in her essay 'Language on loan', states:

> our history of having to learn intrudes. It reminds us of our helplessness and dependency, our fight with authority, as necessary as it may be, and our guilt at having abandoned our earliest loves —our parents and even our omnipotent child selves who could, if only in fantasy, make reality bend to our wishes and believe that infinity is ours to find in the starry night. (40)

In a similar vein to Pitt's claim, Stengel (1939) suggests that acquiring a foreign language is an anachronic act. It is one that sets individuals back to an infantile stage of language learning (476). Learning a new language involves re-experiencing our most primitive history of affect—and thus it uproots learners' feelings of helplessness, dependency, and loss of omnipotence. Along these lines, Stengel suggests that when learning a new language, individuals experience a sense of shame. Such a feeling is emanated when language learners begin to internalize and communicate efficiently in a foreign language (478). Here we may also consider that the guilt or shame learners experience through the transformative act of learning a second language is not only linked to their distancing from their first loves. It is linked to the distancing from their former communities and, by extension, their former selves. Likewise, when addressing learners' host-language acquisition and movement towards the target linguistic-cultural group, Lambert suggests:

> The more proficient one becomes in a second language the more [they] may find that [their] place in [their] original membership group is modified at the same time as the other linguistic-cultural group becomes something more than a reference group for[them]. Depending upon the compatibility of the two cultures, [they] may experience feelings of chagrin or regret as [they lose] ties in one group, mixed with the fearful anticipation of entering a relatively new group. (Lambert 1972: 225, cited in Block 2007: 48)

Lambert's description of this social uncertainty and fear is associated with Émile Durkheim's concept of anomie (Block 2007: 48). This, once again, is

Language Learning and Trauma

Added to the disorientation and the cumulative inner-social crises is the act of significant learning and its unconscious relation to trauma. In 'Pedagogy and clinical knowledge', Britzman and Pitt (2004) explore individuals' unconscious response to new material. Through psychoanalytic and pedagogical lenses, they claim that foreign information which does not align with a learner's schemata can be perceived as 'a force that is not secured by meaning or understanding' (369). For learners, the struggle to comprehend and incorporate unfamiliar information threatens their sense of security and control. This disruption of cognitive frames (Felman 1991: 56) provokes feelings of anxiety and helplessness, which ultimately leads to a crisis. As argued in 'Aggression and the telos of language learning', Britzman and Pitt's (2004) research holds great value in second-language learning, especially for monolingual speakers (Carra-Salsberg 2015a: 37).

With a focus on the emotive nature of the learning process, Britzman and Pitt look at how the interruptions caused by learning, and the disconnect between the old and the new, uproot learners' known and unknown histories (371–72). This unconscious response to the new material gives way to individuals' memories and fantasies of learning and not learning, as well as repression(s) of and resistance(s) to learning. Significant learning, they claim, activates individuals' history of affect and transferences (368–69). Such poorly understood experience, regardless of its connection to the subject's past, is experienced as a force belonging to the present (Klein 1975: 48). Britzman and Pitt contend that once the tension between the learner's inner and outer realities is negotiated between the ego and its environment, symbolization occurs and the learning experience 'is brought into relief through significance' (2004: 369–70, cited in Carra-Salsberg 2015a: 38).

This emphasis on the need for synthesis when learning and becoming transformed through such conscious and unconscious experience is also central to Akhtar's (2012) study of migrants' realities. When studying newcomers' introjection of the new language, Akhtar argues that the new language is only learned when the individual is able to synthesize migration's cumulative

MEMORY WITHIN LANGUAGE

trauma. Until then, he argues, the host language is considered alien, as one that bears no relation to the self (n.p.). Following synthesis, children and adolescents commonly respond to their reality and linguistic condition by absorbing, mastering, and becoming transformed within languages. This eventual acquisition is driven by language learners' inherent and necessary aggression and the universal need to connect and feel included within their immediate environment. Once this occurs, the acquired host tongue becomes appreciated for its symbolic and epistemological nature: for the manner in which it allows its newest speakers the opportunity for psychic growth (Akhtar 1995: 1055). Equally importantly, the new language is also appreciated for the way in which it offers its learners a creative alternative to self-expression (Carra-Salsberg 2015a: 41). Returning to Akhtar, once the host language is encoded and newcomers' sense of linguistic continuity returns, their inner challenges are brought into relief by integrating their trauma and the achievement of 'a comfortable bilingual identity' (Akhtar 2012: n.p.).

Significant Learning, Matricide, and the Re-Creation of the Self

As argued thus far, the initial stages of significant host-language acquisition add to the psycho-emotional, conscious, and unconscious challenges newcomers commonly encounter. The link to speakers' socio-emotional affiliations is also addressed by David Block (2007) in *Second Language Identities*. While discussing Lambert's (1972) work, Block argues that when acquiring and becoming fluid in a host language, learners experience a MODIFICA-TION of membership with the original linguistic-cultural group (Lambert 1972: 22, cited in Block 2007: 48). Such modification, continues Block, leads to chagrin, regret, and moral chaos, which Durkheim terms as anomie (49). Becoming a migrant and learning a host language, asserts Block, implies crossing not only social and geographic borders. Acquiring and internalizing a host language entails the crossing of psychological borders as well (49). Young migrants' acquisition of a host language involves its inevitable internalization. It is a significant act that entails a social and subjective transformation.

A psychoanalytic approach to significant learning is also presented by Jennifer Gilbert (2010) in *Reading Histories: Curriculum Theory, Psychoanalysis,*

CHILD AND ADOLESCENT MIGRATION, MENTAL HEALTH, AND LANGUAGE

and Generational Violence. According to Gilbert, significant learning entails innovation, transformation, murder, and reparation. Gilbert draws from discussions on generational violence, Hannah Arendt's concept of natality, as well as Alice Pitt's and André Green's discussions on reading and its unconscious association to matricide. When examining Green's work, Gilbert quotes: 'To read is to feed off the corpses of one's parents, whom one kills through reading, through the possession of knowledge' (cited in Gilbert 2010: 67). Gilbert associates Green's words with those of Pitt (2006), who, in 'Mother Love's education', suggests that '[r]eading enacts unconscious phantasies of murder and reparation ... an act that is no less violently felt than if an actual murder has taken place' (cited in Gilbert 2010: 67).

According to Gilbert, the phantastical violence that stems from readers' encounters with knowledge alters the learner's sense of self and relationship with their primary caregiver(s) (67). Through the acquisition of knowledge, what drives the child's desire to continue to read and thus introject 'food for the mind' is the unconscious understanding that the primary caregiver(s) survived her child's matricidal act (67–68). Gilbert's arguments are in line with Pitt's (2006) who, in 'Mother Love's education', suggests that matricide is a significant element of every child's development. Acquiring new information moves the child away from their first love objects and times of dependence. This creative replacement, continues Pitt, gives way to the birth of the child's psychic reality and its interconnection with aggression, symbolization, guilt, and need for reparation (87–88).

Pitt argues that the developmental act of matricide is essential to the child's loss of the unspoken self, and transition into language; it is born through and within the child's membership of the wider community of speakers (88–90). As argued in 'Aggression and the telos of learning', 'as unimaginable as these words may seem to readers who are new to psychoanalytic thought, it is not difficult to link this phantasy to any significant learning that entails, by its very influence, a perceived transformation' (Carra-Salsberg 2015a: 39). As argued in this publication, child and adolescent migrants are affected by the conflict that rises from the drastic change in their subject position, and later, from the transformational act of acquiring, introjecting, and relating within a new host language. These subjective and social shifts create a conscious and unconscious conflict that adds to newcomers' guilt and sense of cumulative crises.

Stigma and the Conceptualization of the Foreign Other: An Added Challenge to Migrants' Experiences

While acquiring a host language may create a strain between children and their caregivers, so does the stress that stems from being targets of prejudice and discrimination. This book's first chapter took a semiotic approach to the study of how social constructions knowingly and unknowingly become accentuated and canonized by individuals. It argued that such partial or full internalization of belief systems is a natural by-product of ongoing social interactions. These negotiations of meaning affect individuals' self–other conceptualizations, identity formations, and ongoing relations with members of their immediate and extended circles. This section complements the book's first chapter, while continuing with this chapter's focus on the developmental challenges that young migrants and families experience. It thus turns our attention to migrants' response to the stigma commonly attached to migration.

As claimed by Major and O'Brien, 'stigma exists when [widely shared] labeling, negative stereotyping, exclusion, discrimination, and low status co-occur in a power situation that allows these processes to unfold' (Link & Phelan 2001, cited in Major & O'Brien 2005: 395). It is a collective, social construction that unfairly devalues individuals who share common characteristics. Characteristics may involve physical traits, country or region of origin, shared histories, religion, and ethnicity. This form of discrimination may be conceptualized through evolutionary and psychoanalytic interpretations.

According to evolutionist scholars, excluding people who possess specific attributes is part of societies' cognitive adaptation. As argued by Major and O'Brien, this tribal behaviour has a functional dimension that is intended to help the group survive. Such attributes include perceiving specific groups as disfavoured partners for social exchange, bearers of parasitic infections, or individuals who can be easily exploited for in-group gain (395). Yet from a psychoanalytic perspective, the 'us versus them', 'insider versus outsider' instincts, as well as individuals' fear of those perceived as foreign, may be linked to subjects' psychological development.

As argued by Volkan (2017), the concept of the foreign–other dichotomy begins at infancy when children introject their primary caregiver's image. The internal image of caregivers and members of children's immediate environment becomes a differential—us versus them—marker. By eight months of age children's recognition that not all faces around them belong to their caregivers gives rise to the psychoanalytic phenomenon known as 'stranger danger'. The anxiety that develops towards strangers, continues Volkan, is a normal part of children's growth, and becomes 'the foundation of evolution of normal prejudice' (86). Race may not be the only characteristic that marks migrants as 'foreigners' among members of the transit or host country. As is common with unconscious responses, this form of othering becomes generalized. It may extend to groups' differing ethnicity, religion, language, and histories. The latter becomes most evident with survivors of trauma.[9]

The problem with stigma is that it not only affects individuals' social interactions with members of their immediate and extended environments. Since it is born from hegemonic relations of power, the threat affecting those targeted is systemic. As such, it may affect marginalized groups within the realms of employment, healthcare, education, law enforcement, and policymaking. As stressed in Chapter 1, the stigma attached to migration influences countries' international laws, receiving systems, as well as available resources and programmes that are meant to aid in newcomers' positive adjustment. When focusing on children and adolescent migrants we should consider that the devaluation of and lack of trust towards migrants not only trigger an affective, cognitive, physiological, and behavioural response from those who are targeted (394, 402). Stigma affects young migrants' subject position and self-esteem. Furthermore, it may also impact on young migrants' education, academic performance, and life outcomes.

Conclusion

This chapter argued that an internalized language is a phenomenon that forms and informs our cognitive and social growth. It studied how this unique human trait allows us to communicate and establish socio-emotional ties with those who form part of our third space. It also examined how a first language or mother tongue is a singularity that becomes grounded within our known and consciously forgotten infantile memories. As such, it is a link to our history of affect and subjective development. This chapter also looked at how our mother tongue is part of a paradox that aids in our separation-individuation from and connection with our primary caregivers, and our awareness—and othering—of the world that surrounds them.

MEMORY WITHIN LANGUAGE

The psychoanalytic theories discussed in this chapter focus on a primary and a later tongue's affective and developmental significance. Through them we have highlighted how a language's development is concurrent with that of the ego. Through a psychoanalytic lens, this chapter investigated how an internalized symbolic code bears the emotional traces of individuals' poorly remembered yet deeply felt histories. It focused on the manner in which children, adolescents, and adults use language to introject, identify, individuate, conceptualize, and feel loved through the establishment of primary and later object relations. By emphasizing the affective, psychological, and socio-developmental significance of a first language, this chapter shed light onto the inner challenges children and adolescents encounter when immersed within the compounds of a foreign language. It brought into conversation how the traumas individuals may experience before their relocation and/or during their migration journey often become compounded with the cumulative inner crises that are born from: 1) becoming suddenly immersed into a foreign language and culture, 2) their sudden shift in subject position, 3) the process of significant learning, and 4) the challenges that stem from becoming targets of stigma.

While the first two challenges are linked to discussions offered in this book's previous chapter, this current chapter looked at the psycho-affective concerns associated with learning. It stressed how myelinization and fear of appearing comic influence the acquisition of a language. It explored how significant host-language learning becomes a transformational occurrence that uproots learners' history of affect and history of learning. It drew attention to the inner conflicts and crises that stem from learning. It also examined how when presented with new material, learners are plunged into a state of confusion that stems from needing to symbolize material that is yet to be secured by meaning. This chapter highlighted how acquiring a new language resubmits learners to an infantile stage of language learning. In line with the unconscious law of relationality, it noted how such resubmission lends to the uprooting of the ego's earliest inarticulate emotions that become juxtaposed with fears, anxieties, and a need for independence (Carra-Salsberg 2015a: 48).

This chapter addressed how the sudden immersion into a new language and community of speakers is also reminiscent of the crisis infants experience through their introduction to their primary language, the Symbolic Order, and the greater community of speakers. Added to such conflicts is the ego's interpretation of learning, as an act that becomes unconsciously perceived as matricidal. Such interpretation substantiates the foundation of language learners' sensed conflict and feeling of 'anomie' or guilt. This chapter stressed how significant language learning involves replacing one's primary symbolic code with the code of the Other. It also involves introjecting belief systems that may challenge those held by newcomers' primary caregivers.

Along with Chapter 1, this chapter also paid close attention to how stigma, racism, and discrimination affects migrant groups. It drew attention to the manner in which widely spread prejudice affects migrants at the affective, cognitive, physiological, and behavioural levels (Major & O'Brien 2005: 394, 402). Equally importantly, it highlighted its far-reaching impact on child and adolescent migrants' social interactions and affiliations, mental health, and family dynamics. This chapter stressed how adults' ongoing struggles may deepen minors' resentment towards their caregivers' decision to migrate (Carra-Salsberg 2017: 21). It, once again, studied how the stigma associated with migration increases the strain within a family's dynamics, and how it may deepen children's desire to individuate, and break away from a label that perhaps makes young migrants feel devalued and othered.

With a continued focus on international migrations, the following chapter pays close attention to theories of trauma. It also takes a psychoanalytic approach to the study of childhood and adolescence and draws attention to the importance of minors' home environments during such developmental stages. The chapter studies how accompanied and unaccompanied migrants' needs and psycho-emotional challenges differ greatly as they navigate through the complexity of their unique conditions and resulting cumulative crises.

4 Trauma's Dimension within and outside Language

> Trust in language is the opposite—distrust of language—situated within language. Confidence in language is language itself distrusting—defying—language: finding in its own space the unshakable principles of a critique. Whence the recourse of etymology (or the refusal to acknowledge any value in it); whence the appeal to anagrammatical entertainments, to acrobatic inversions whose intent is to multiply words infinitively on the pretext of deforming them, but in vain. All this is justified on the condition that it all (recourse and refusal) be employed at once, at the same time, without belief in any of it, and without cease. The unknown of language remains unknown—the stranger foreign.
>
> (Blanchot 1995: 38)

Given the focus of this chapter and book, it seems fitting to begin our discussion on trauma and on the significance of language and writing by considering Blanchot's words. At first glance, one might suggest that this French theorist and literary critic highlights the ambiguity of language by stressing how words may capture a multitude of intended and unintended meanings. Some may argue that this passage brings to light the ways in which significations become formed, informed, deformed, exposed, and sometimes hidden, depending on contexts, intent, histories, interpretations, and insights. By looking at this writer's own history of trauma, many may also suggest that Blanchot's disjointed yet carefully chosen expression is grounded in his attempt to express his confounded reality within a lived trauma.

Blanchot's desire to write, testify, and conceptualize retrospective aspects of his life were born from his personal and shared experiences. During World War II, his vocalized political beliefs as a columnist and critic led to his arrest, and to the subsequent trauma of standing in front of a Nazi firing squad. Following this horrifying occurrence, which he later called 'the instance of his death', Blanchot's concerns were magnified when, by the end of the war, he learned the extent of the atrocities involving Europe's concentration camps. These experiences of war led to Blanchot's voluntary isolation in a remote cabin. Alone, in such dwelling, this political, philosophical, and critical thinker chose writing as the medium to express and exemplify his trauma(s).

In 'Beyond the pleasure principle', Freud (2006) claims that victims of distressing events demonstrate a fixation with the moment of a traumatic occurrence. This is because, frequently, survivors feel temporarily fixed in a non-integrated state of confusion. Many feel the need to repeatedly describe their fixation in the hope of understanding and/or releasing themselves from the after-effects of their haunting experience (139). For Blanchot (1995), his traumatic history led to a quest for meaning and representation through his writing, which he refers to as 'the friendship of the ill'. His written expression embodies an attempt to convey and symbolize that which cannot be fully verbalized, and 'cannot be made evident ... [for it] escapes every possible utterance' (Blanchot 1995: 38). Equally importantly, Blanchot's relentless obsession with testifying to an inconceivable truth unfolds a theory—one that represents his experience of existential threat and interruption of a linear sense of history. Here we find the 'atomic threat' (Freud 2006: 118–19) that engulfed his past, haunted his present, and denied him the ability to conceptualize a future. In other words, through his confounding writing, Blanchot offers his readers a glimpse of the fragmentation of his existence.

Within the intra- and inter-subjective world of language and founded on the Hegelian principle, Blanchot (1995) destructs to construct or *reconstruct* (Blanchot 1995: 119, emphasis added) the conceptualizations rendered from his experiences. Unlike memoirs that depict the singular voice of survivors, Blanchot's *Writing of the Disaster* is, as expressed by Éric Hoppenot (2014), 'more than a writing of survivors ... [it] is a place where revenants express themselves. A ghostly language that has incorporated the voice of those who have disappeared ... [Blanchot's] writing of the disaster is where the ashes of those who remain without a grave are buried' (193). Equally importantly, Blanchot's work highlights the significance of writing. Specifically, it stresses the importance of bearing witness to horrifying events that rest outside the parameters of reason.

Amid his voluntary isolation, Blanchot breaches his silence and establishes a connection to the rest of the world through writing. Even though his work for the most part addresses an anonymous audience, it directly and indirectly draws attention to the value of human connectedness, to our universal desire to be heard, conceptualize, and feel understood.

With a continued focus on trauma, the socio-developmental importance of human connectedness, and the concerns affecting many child and adolescent migrants, this chapter begins with an examination of the significance of parental figures for children. It studies how, during childhood, the presence or absence of primary caregivers impacts individuals' experiences and long-term coping mechanisms. Specific to migrants, their ability or inability to cope often translates into difficulties amalgamated with the challenges imposed by their pre- and post-relocation experiences. This chapter also looks closely at the different types of traumas that often affect child/adolescent migrants and their parents.

A Psychoanalytic Examination of the Short- and Long-Term Significance of Parental Figures during Childhood and Adolescence

Over the years, psychoanalysis has centred much of its attention on the developmental importance of primary caregivers' involvement in children's psychosexual and emotional growth. This focus on the significance of a healthy home environment has been central to Sigmund Freud's work. It is read, for example, in the well-known, and often misunderstood, theory of the Oedipal Complex. Through this theory, Freud highlights how a child establishes early and later lifelong emotional attachments through their interaction with their parents. According to Freud, the child's successful negotiation of this complex results in the establishment of the incest barrier, and the child's acceptance of generational boundaries and transition from the pleasure principle to the reality principle (Akhtar 2009: 197). This early experience, continues Freud, establishes the foundation of the child's personality development, and induces the formation of the individual's reality as a split subject.

The significance of a mother or maternal figure in the child's socio-emotional development is also examined by Anna Freud (1998a). In 'Observations on child development', Anna Freud studies the importance of a child's fusion of their aggressive and libidinal drives. She argues that, between twelve and eighteen months, the stimulant for libidinal development is the child's relationship

CHILD AND ADOLESCENT MIGRATION, MENTAL HEALTH, AND LANGUAGE

with their mother. When such a relationship is impaired or missing, the child's emotional development is stunted. Through her work, Anna Freud stresses that in the unfortunate event of a parent's death, or a parent's sudden inability to be emotionally present, the child often experiences a regression of their most recent ego achievements. Depending on the child's age, she continues, regression may involve speech, locomotion, and overt displays of aggression. Achievements that are necessary for a child's normal development such as sublimation, idealization, and social adaptation may also be affected (58–61).

With attention to the primitive mental activity of infants, in her publication with Joan Riviere, Melanie Klein (1964) also studies the importance of a healthy child–parent relationship. Specifically, she pays close attention to the positive and negative feelings that arise within the child as a result of their mother's response to their fundamental need to be nourished. According to Klein, at the onset of postnatal life, infants experience powerful impulses of gratitude and love when nourished, and frustration along with hate when hungry. She stresses that since the mother's breast or bottle becomes the object that provides the infant with nourishment and sensual pleasure, the child's feelings of love and hate are first experienced towards the breasts or bottle and later towards the mother as a person (59–60). When experiencing hate, argues Klein, the infant is governed by aggressive forces and phantasies of harm and destruction, which, in the child's unconscious mind, become interpreted as real, as if actual harm has taken place (61). Thus, once the child is once again nourished, along with the infant's sense of gratitude come feelings of guilt and a need for reparation (57–58).

According to Kleinian thought, not only does a mother's ability to eventually comfort and nourish gives her child a sense of security and a feeling of being loved, but a primary caregiver's attention and nourishment triggers within the child an unconscious concern and guilt over the damage that, in the child's unconscious mind, has taken place. Klein stresses that a child's phantastical aggression, resulting guilt, and unconscious need for reparation are important for the child's growth. When concerned over the well-being of their mother, the child not only develops omnipotent phantasies of the repairing or healing kind, but the child's fear of harm and unconscious guilt also makes them love and appreciate their primary caregiver at a deeper level.

For the child, this infantile experience lays the grounds for their capacity for love. Commonly, this faculty becomes extended to the father or secondary

72

TRAUMA'S DIMENSION WITHIN AND OUTSIDE LANGUAGE

caregiver and becomes eventually transferred to those who play a significant role in the child's life. As claimed by Klein:

> Because our mother first satisfied all of our self-preservative needs and sensual desires and gave us security, the part she plays in our mind is a lasting one ... The very important part the father plays in the child's emotional life also influences all later love relations, and all other human associations. But the baby's early relation to him, in so far as he is felt as a gratifying, friendly, and protective figure is partly modelled on the one of the mother. (59)

As highlighted in this book's previous chapter, Donald Winnicott (2005) has also studied the manner in which children's pattern of emotional growth develops through their interactions with their primary caregiver. In his discussion of the developmental significance of a transitional object, Winnicott stresses that when children are provided with a good enough holding environment, they learn to love, individuate, and live creatively. In *Home Is Where We Start From*, Winnicott (1986) stresses that a person's ability to develop emotionally and live creatively begins during childhood when the home environment allows for the child to fee sense of omnipotence, and thus an impression that they can create their world. Even though the world pre-existed the infant, within this good enough environment, the child is made to believe they created it. This belief of omnipotence, which is, once again, attained through the infant's interaction with their mother, is crucial to their future relationships, perceptions, and behaviours. Once the child begins to use words, they experience a play between omnipotence and compliance. The latter is born from their acceptance of the reality principle. When this occurs, the child learns that they must adapt to their external world (40). Yet despite the child's acknowledgement of the reality principle and hence their learned need to comply, that inner sense of omnipotence and sense of being able to create a new world—or to see things anew—remain. It is through such a sense, claims Winnicott, that the individual lives creatively.

Living creatively is not the same as creating art. Yet art cannot be created without the remanence of the child's feeling of omnipotence, and hence individuals' sense of being able to bring into existence something new (43). Creativity, argues Winnicott, 'belongs to being alive' (41). It is about reaching out for an object—physically and/or mentally—to establish a relationship. It involves certain mechanisms of projection and introjection, and thus the functions of identifying oneself with others and the other with oneself (47). Creative living is interlinked with the development of new relationships while retaining something personal that is unmistakably part of the self. The infant is predisposed to find a world of objects and ideas (49). It is a universal need and universal experience that is 'more important than eating or than physical survival'. It is key to being happy, even if anxiety drives the artist's brand of creativity (44).

Adolescence, Turmoil, and their Unquestionable Link to Teenagers' Childhood Histories

Adolescence extends from a child's latency period until adulthood (A. Freud 1998c: 192). While the former is characterized by a period of decreased libidinal and aggressive impulses, adolescence is a stage marked by inner turmoil. This stage, argues Anna Freud, is one of anxiety outbreaks, neurotic behaviour, and increased ego defence. It is 'an interruption of peaceful growth', for it is charged with emotional upsets and structural upheavals (195). Anna Freud describes adolescence as a stage characterized by the breakdown of infantile morality. This breakdown, she suggests, is linked to the breakthrough from individuals' repressed instinctual life. During this necessary developmental period, children often feel inhibited, depressed, and at variance with their environment (172–74). The conflicting feelings that affect the child during adolescence are also stressed by Melanie Klein. When discussing this developmental period, Klein and Riviere (1964) describes it as a stage that challenges both children and their parents. With adolescents, they continue, parents' patience and their capacity to love and understand their children are tested.

When studying adolescence in psychoanalytic literature, Anna Freud draws attention to her father's publication *Three Essays on the Theory of Sexuality*. As stated by Sigmund Freud (1905), puberty is 'the period that gives infantile sexual life its final shape'. During this stage, he highlights, the main events include 'subordination of the erotogenic zones to the primacy of the genital zone; the setting up of new sexual aims, and the finding of new sexual objects outside of the family' (cited in A. Freud 1998b: 183). Central to Anna Freud's discussion, adolescents' experiences are affected by their history of infantile development. During this stage of confusion and 'bewilderment', claims Anna Freud, pre-existing methods of defence are brought into play and strained, as the ego and superego alter to accommodate the new, mature forms of sexuality (183–86).

TRAUMA'S DIMENSION WITHIN AND OUTSIDE LANGUAGE

By examining Ernest Jones' (1922) paper on 'Some problems of adolescence', Anna Freud continues to draw attention to the significant relation between adolescence and infancy. She cites Jones' statement that 'the period between the ages of 2 and 5 must be regarded as an important precursor of the subsequent final organization'. Continuing to cite Jones, Anna Freud highlights that during this final stage of development, the individual recapitulates and expands what they passed through during the first five years of life (183).

The link between adolescence and children's first years of life, and the former's progression from such individuals' early defences, is also addressed in Klein's and Riviere's (1964) publication. In Klein's section, also titled 'Love, guilt and reparation', Klein examines adolescents' libido displacement. According to Klein, during adolescence, since 1) repressed conflicts and sexual desires connected with their parents begin to once again gain strength, and 2) teenagers' early, unconscious feelings of rivalry and hatred against their parents are awoken and 'experienced in full force', adolescents turn away from their parents in an attempt to break free from the overbearing love, hate, and rivalry that, since childhood, had become repressed (96–97). As observed by Anna Freud, when adolescents experience the anxiety aroused by the attachment to their infantile love object, instead of permitting the process of gradual detachment, they suddenly withdraw their libido from them. Even though their motives remain unconscious, this act leaves adolescents with a passionate longing for partnership. This longing, continues Klein, is what draws teenagers to transfer their libido to subsequent love objects (196).

Along such lines, in her publication with Riviere, Klein argues that even though the hate adolescents often experience towards their parents may also be extended to people such as teachers and schoolmates,[1] adolescents' attachment to parent substitutes is guided by individuals' universal need to preserve goodness and love. To counterbalance their negative feelings, 'the aggressive youth is ... driven to find people who [they] can look up to and idealize' (96). This explains why adolescents' feelings are those of either hero worship and love, or displacement, hate and/or scorn (79–80, 91). The love felt within adolescent friendships becomes a safeguard against hatred. Yet since adolescents experience an increased strength and intensity in impulses, teenagers' friendships tend to remain unstable (98–99). This may be especially true when the attachment or friendship is established with contemporaries who form part of adolescent groups.

Added to the 'defense by displacement of libido', Anna Freud brings forth a second unconscious response against infantile love objects: 'defense by reversal of affect'. With this defence, instead of displacing libido from parents—or after failing to do so—the adolescent ego may defend itself by turning the emotions felt towards the parents to the opposite. This defence incurs 'the change from love to hate, dependence into revolt, respect and admiration into contempt and derision' (198). With such a reversal of affect the adolescent imagines themselves to be free. Such freedom, argues Anna Freud, is superficial. At the unconscious level, the adolescent remains tied to paternal figures. Hence, acting out remains within the family environment. There is only suffering. In other words, the individual experiences no positive pleasures from the reversed relationships, no independence of action or of growth. Anxiety and guilt remain, and thus 'constant reinforcement of the defense is necessary' (198). This is provided, continues Anna Freud, by two methods: denial—of positive feelings—and reaction formations—rude, unsympathetic, condescending attitudes (198–99). Further pathological developments include hostility and aggressiveness—defence against object love, which becomes intolerable to the ego and experienced as a threat. This may take place in the form of projection—aggression directed at parents, who are sensed as the main oppressors and persecutors. On the other hand, the full hostility and aggression may be turned away from the first objects of affection and turned inwards against the self. In such cases the adolescent displays depression, tendency towards self-injury, and, in extreme cases, suicidal wishes (199).

Two other defences noted by Anna Freud are the 'defense by withdrawal of libido to the self' and 'defense by regression'. Following the withdrawal of libido from the parents, if anxieties and inhibitions are not directed to new objects outside the family, the libido remains within the self. This, in turn, may inflate the ego and superego. Hence, ideas of grandeur may appear, along with fantasies of unlimited power over others: 'the suffering and persecuted ego of the adolescent may assume Christlike proportions with corresponding fantasies of saving the world' (199–200). Or the cathexis may become attached only to the adolescent's body and give rise to hypochondriacal sensations and feelings of body changes (200). For the latter defence, 'defense by regression', the greater the anxiety caused by the object ties, the more primitive is the teenager's defence activity to escape them. Hence, we see regressive changes in all aspects of the teenager's personality—in ego and libido organization. Ego

TRAUMA'S DIMENSION WITHIN AND OUTSIDE LANGUAGE

boundaries are widened. This entails changes in the teenager's qualities, attitudes, and outward appearance. Projections and identifications are prevalent and create a give and take between the self and the object, which has repercussions on ego functions. For example, reality testing and the distinction between the inner and outer world is affected. There is a lapse in ego functioning and a state of confusion (200–01). Here we see a fear of emotional surrender and a fear of loss of identity (201).

During adolescence, disharmony within the psyche structure is a fact. There are battles between the id and ego. Defensive methods employed are either against impulses or against object cathexis (200). It is normal for an adolescent to behave in an unpredictable manner, to fight and accept impulses, to love and hate parents, to revolt against and depend on them, to be ashamed of their mother before others and to desire heart-to-heart talks with her. An adolescent thrives on imitation of and identification with others while searching for their own identity. Fluctuations between extreme opposites are deemed abnormal during any other time in life, but normal during adolescence.

As argued thus far, adolescents' behaviours are inconsistent and unpredictable. The extreme fluctuations and difficulties presented during this stage gives us an insight into why, according to Anna Freud, parents, more than adolescents, need guidance (203–04). While the developmental period of adolescence challenges most caregivers, this stage may, once again, be especially trying for migrant parents, who may already be overburdened by their past histories and cumulative crises. If we look at migrants' reality from the perspective of the child, we must also note that the challenges and extenuating circumstances undergone by—documented and undocumented—adults and children also have a direct impact on young and older children's development. When parents are physically and/or emotionally absent, children's interpersonal relations, ongoing defences and ability or inability to thrive and adapt in a new, confounding environment and host language become affected.

By choosing at least one of the adaptive solutions, or libido directions, the adolescent feels free as they enjoy the new sense of independence from parents who 'are treated with indifference bordering on callousness'. Even though such a shift in libido directions is normal, the suddenness of change, contrast in object selection, and overemphasis on new alliances mark this common teenage act as defensive, instead of a normal developmental process. As parents become less important to the adolescent because of this removal of cathexis from them,

CHILD AND ADOLESCENT MIGRATION, MENTAL HEALTH, AND LANGUAGE

the teenager's guilt, and anxiety—the internal conflicts—decrease, and the ego becomes more tolerant. This is due to the ceasing of pregenital and genital impulses, previously linked to the child's parents. Here we see an inner rearrangement or a new transference of object love, whereby formerly repressed sexual and aggressive impulses or wishes are acted upon with individuals that exist outside the adolescent's family environment. As claimed by Anna Freud, depending on the love object to which the teenager has attached, the acting out is either harmless, idealistic, dissocial, or criminal (197–98).

Childhood, Adolescence, and Migration

As argued thus far, attention to the presence or absence of children's parents is essential to our study of children's and adolescents' short- and long-term socio-emotional and sexual development. Home environments lay the foundations for the complexity of all interpersonal relations and behaviours throughout life, as well as individuals' ongoing perceptions. Being raised in a supportive home allows for the child to develop the necessary tools to establish healthy emotional connections and thrive and adapt to usual and unusual challenges. With this in mind, since geographic, linguistic, and/or cultural migrations encompass an accumulation of stressful, life-changing events, paying attention to children's developmental history is key to our study of child and adolescent migration and mental health.

In the chapter 'Rites of passage in migration and adolescence: struggling in transformation', Celia Enriquez de Salamanca (2020) discusses a case of a fourteen-year-old child migrant, Alicia, who relocated with her mother and stepfather from Latin America to Germany. Concerns over this patient were centred on her lack of self-esteem, depression, thoughts of suicide, and anger. Alicia seemed unable to establish positive relationships at school and to embrace her new life in Germany. During therapy sessions, Alicia would only speak Spanish, her mother tongue. According to Alicia, her unwillingness to communicate in the host language were founded on her aversion to sounding foreign. Enriquez de Salamanca established that Alicia's challenges exceeded the typical stressors she encountered as an adolescent and a newcomer. According to this analyst, Alicia's anger and the challenges she encountered prior to and following her relocation were rooted in her infantile history of object relations (113–16).

TRAUMA'S DIMENSION WITHIN AND OUTSIDE LANGUAGE

As a child, Alicia felt abandoned by her mother and forced to live with her grandparents. Eventually, when 'her grandparents became too old and sick to take care of her', Alicia was uprooted from her childhood home and, while leaving her grandparents behind, she was made to migrate with her mother and stepfather to Germany (115–16). As argued by Enriquez de Salamanca, Alicia's anger, sense of loss, and inability to adjust and thrive within a facilitating external environment were not only founded on her migration and feeling that she had been 'kidnapped by her own mother and driven into exile' (114). Her unhappiness was also attributed to challenges that were rooted in early object relations (114). Alicia's emotional insecurity and self-devaluation were grounded on her history of confounding loss. From a Kleinian perspective, one could agree that during childhood, Alicia's mother's absence annulled Alicia's needed development of narcissistic gratification. As a child, Alicia did not experience her mother's love and resulting sense of emotional security (115). This, in turn, affected Alicia's short- and long-term development. For the latter, it influenced her ability to connect with others at an emotional level.

We may consider that Alicia's perceptions and behaviours are also rooted in ego psychology. Beginning with the reflexive process of projection, as claimed by Anna Freud (1936), through this mechanism of defence, unwanted wishes and/or feelings individuals attribute to another person are felt as if they were directed towards the self (24). For Alicia, since she was denied a healthy parent–child relation, the hatred and discontent she felt towards her first love object became displaced to later substitutes. Naturally, this affected her relationship with others, transforming this hate she felt towards those around her into a conviction that she herself was hated. Another unconscious defence Alicia may have employed is 'turning against the self'. As one of nine mechanisms described by Anna Freud (7), through this method the ego injures or places the self at a disadvantage. This may explain why Alicia was involved in toxic relationships, was unable to stand up for herself at school, and was affected by thoughts of suicide.

Finally, we cannot disregard the power and developmental significance of transference. For Alicia, her inability to establish healthy and stable attachments with those who form part of her immediate social settings is a repetition of her earliest partnership—or lack of partnership—with her mother, and absent father. Alicia's choice of language may also be linked to transference. We should bear in mind that the feelings one has for one's first love are not solely transferred to other people; they may also be transferred to inanimate objects (Klein & Riviere 1964: 91). Alicia's unwillingness to express herself in German is not limited to her fear of sounding foreign. As she blames her mother for having relocated to Germany, such a refusal is linked, at least in part, to her feelings towards her mother and her mother's substitutes. Even though a mother tongue is commonly linked to the maternal imago (Akhtar 2012: n.p.), for Alicia, her first language is also reminiscent of her childhood home and life with her grandparents. Hence, while Spanish is connected to the remembered, imagined, or idealized safety her grandparents afforded her, German becomes associated with her mother's choices. For Alicia, this later language represents the newly imposed environment she openly rejects.

As highlighted by Enriquez de Salamanca, added to the problems that were rooted in her childhood history, her patient's challenges and perception of reality also stem from 'a two-fold migration': 1) her migration to a new country with a new language and an unknown culture, and 2) her migration to the turbulent inner and external world of puberty (116).

Migration and Trauma

As stressed in this book's second chapter, both unaccompanied and accompanied minors are frequently affected by cumulative crises taking place before, during, and/or following their relocations. Unfortunately, it is not uncommon to hear of the link between migration and trauma. While some minors may be affected by wars, unwanted separations, or the death of loved ones, others may be impacted by the dangers of clandestine border crossings or subjected to the unwelcoming and often terrifying conditions encountered in refugee camps.

Following their move to transit and/or host countries, both documented and undocumented migrants may also be impacted by cumulative stressors that stem from unwelcoming receiving systems, and/or by the psycho-emotional and financial concerns incurred as they attempt to adjust to their lives as new migrants. While people migrate in the hopes of better opportunities, it is not unusual for newcomers to mourn their past lives and the people they left behind. Unaccompanied minors may also feel unprotected and struggle within countries, cultures, and novel circumstances they may hardly understand.

TRAUMA'S DIMENSION WITHIN AND OUTSIDE LANGUAGE

Documented and undocumented accompanied minors, meanwhile, may be affected by their primary caregivers' stresses and psychic condition.

A Note on Trauma

In examining the link between migrancy and trauma, we must consider the latter's definition as a phenomenon caused by an unprecedented and highly stressful occurrence. It is one that poses 'a [perceptual] threat to the physical [and psychological] integrity of the self' (Luckhurst 2008: 1). A trauma is classified as impersonal or interpersonal, depending on the source or nature of the incident(s). Fowler et al. (2013) suggest that while both impersonal and interpersonal experiences are caused by external events, an impersonal trauma is unrelated to human interactions. Examples of impersonal traumas are those engendered by natural disasters or accidents, such as near-drowning experiences and vehicle collisions. Interpersonal traumas, on the other hand, result from the extreme stress evoked by the threatening behaviours of others. Such traumas stem from direct exposure to violence, the act of witnessing violence (313), or individuals' response to learning about others' experiences within violence (Felman & Laub 1992: 48; Luckhurst 2008: 2–3, 7–8).

Trauma's transmissibility is highlighted by Roger Luckhurst (2008) when he states:

> [Trauma] leaks between mental and physical symptoms, between patients, patients and doctors via ... transference or suggestion and between victims and their listeners or viewers who are commonly moved to forms of overwhelming sympathy, even to the extent of claiming secondary victimhood. (3)

Luckhurst emphasizes that the infectious quality of trauma has led to the classification of victims' status as primary or secondary. As such, primary victim status is ascribed to those who lived through an impersonal or interpersonal trauma. On the other hand, secondary trauma is attributed to individuals who become overwhelmed by others' experiences. Examples of the latter are witnesses, bystanders, rescue workers, individuals touched by the immediate aftermath of a trauma, and even those receiving news of death or injury of a relative or loved one (1–2).

A confounding characteristic of this phenomenon lies in the subjective disturbance that rises not just from its onset—that is, the original traumatic

CHILD AND ADOLESCENT MIGRATION, MENTAL HEALTH, AND LANGUAGE

moment—but also from its symptoms. When looking at current descriptions of post-traumatic stress disorder (PTSD), we learn that a traumatic event is not commonly registered at the conscious level. Instead, it becomes unconsciously imprinted. While consciously inaccessible and seemingly forgotten by the subject, the scene of trauma often re-emerges belatedly through recurrent flashbacks, nightmares, and/or intrusive thoughts. Such unexpected manifestations, along with somatic sensations and behavioural re-enactments, commonly occur when the individual is exposed to a situation that resembles the original scene (163, 172, 174, 176).

When post-traumatic manifestations occur, they bring individuals back to the original scene, leaving them in a reawakened state of confusion, increased fright, and dread of reoccurrence.

Trauma and Memory

When addressing trauma's unusual memory registration, Cathy Caruth (1995) suggests:

> The flashbacks [and the overall intrusive reliving of traumatic memory] ... provide a form of recall that survives at the cost of willed memory or of the very continuity of conscious thought. While the traumatized are called upon to see and to relive the insistent reality of the past, they recover a past that encounters consciousness only through the very denial of active recollection.
>
> The ability to recover the past is thus closely and paradoxically tied up, in trauma, with the inability to have access to it. And this suggests that what returns in the flashbacks, [nightmares, and intrusive thoughts] is not simply an overwhelming experience that has been obstructed by a later ... amnesia, but an event that is itself constituted, in part, by its lack of integration into consciousness. (152)

From a neurobiological perspective, van der Kolk and van der Hart (1995) claim that dissociation that results from an individual's inability to recall the traumatic scene occurs when the experience does not fit into the sufferer's pre-existing schemas. Their argument is based on the findings of Piaget (1962), who suggests:

> It is precisely because there is no immediate accommodation that there is complete dissociation of the inner activity from the external world. As

TRAUMA'S DIMENSION WITHIN AND OUTSIDE LANGUAGE

the external world is solely represented by images, it is assimilated without resistance (i.e., unattached to other memories) to the unconscious ego. They therefore cannot be easily translated into the symbolic language necessary for linguistic retrieval. (Cited in van der Kolk & van der Hart 1995: 172–73)

When comparing narrative or ordinary memory with that of trauma, we note a stark contrast in processing and registration. Beginning with ordinary memory, this mentation is a flexible and adaptable constructive process. A non-traumatic event is automatically encoded, categorized, and stored within schemas or pre-existing frameworks of experience (van der Kolk and van der Hart 1995: 163, 169). As such, the memory becomes integrated with previous recollections that are automatically and unconsciously interpreted as similar. Such storage and integration explains the common inaccuracy of an ordinary memory during retrieval. Since similar memories are stored together, it becomes difficult for the individual to differentiate old information from new or newer examples (van der Kolk & van der Hart 1995: 170–71).[2]

Schacter (2001) offers a different perspective on ordinary memory—one that highlights the affective influence of its layered construction and eventual retrieval. He claims:

Our memories work differently from the way a camera records. We extract key elements from our experiences and store them. We then recreate or reconstruct our experiences rather than retrieve copies of them. Sometimes, in the process of reconstructing, we add on feelings, beliefs, or even knowledge we obtained after the experience. In other words, we bias our memories of the past by attributing to them emotions or knowledge we acquire after the event. (Cited in Tuters 2016: n.p.)

Schacter (2001), as well as van der Kolk and van der Hart (1995), note that even though recall and reconstruction of events are voluntary acts, the storage of ordinary memories is a part of an automatic process—one that is influenced by individuals' cumulative experiences, knowledge, and interrelated emotions.

A breakdown of differentiable memory systems is offered by Joseph Fernando (2022) in his discussion of trauma. Memories, he claims, include implicit memory (learned unconsciously from the basic spatial orientation of the environment), procedural memory (learned motor actions), semantic memory (linked with knowledge), episodic or explicit memory (perceptual), affective or emotional memory, and narrative or autobiographical memory. Fernando argues that the latter involves an integration of episodic, semantic, and verbal memory. He distinguishes between episodic and narrative (or verbal) memory and contends that narrative memory is torn apart and suppressed during trauma. Specifically, he explains, during traumatic and stressful times, episodic memory remains unintegrated and unsymbolized, appearing 'quite raw by comparison to regular episodic memory' (n.p.).

Distinctions between different types of memories and attention to that of trauma also appears, again, in the work of Caruth (1995). Guided by Janet's writing, Caruth suggests that while familiar occurrences become integrated within individuals' conscious framework of experiences, frightening, novel, or extraordinary events are not properly or automatically processed by the Central Nervous System (CNS). When exposed to a traumatic occurrence, individuals are left in a state of shock or 'speechless fright'. Since they cannot organize and process the trauma linguistically, the anxiety-evoking scene becomes registered at a somato-sensory or iconic level as a fragmentary experience. When this occurs, the event is either remembered with particular vividness, or is consciously unavailable for voluntary recall. Consequently, Caruth posits, 'fragments of these unintegrated experiences may later manifest in recollections or behavioural re-enactments' (159-60, 171).

What matters most to our discussion is that, unlike ordinary memory, the recollection of a traumatic event often becomes fixed and unaffected by the usual distortions of conscious recall (Caruth 1995: 153; Fernando 2022: n.p.).

Furthermore, this focus on the pathologic registration of traumatic memory is key to our understanding of the constellation of symptoms that add to trauma's unsettling quality. These include—yet are not limited to—the sufferers' sense of helplessness and depression (Kronick, Rousseau & Cleveland 2018: 425), as well as emotional numbness (Freud 1920: 13; Luckhurst 2008: 1). On the opposite end of the symptomological spectrum, individuals may also respond to trauma by experiencing a consistent loss of temper control, and hypervigilance or 'exaggerated startle response' (Luckhurst 2008: 1). Likewise, sufferers either avoid thoughts and/or feelings associated with the trauma(s) or become fixated on the moment(s) of the significant occurrence(s) (Freud 1920: 13).

Newcomers' Preconscious Experiences of Trauma

At a 2012 conference entitled *Strange Lands: Location and Dislocation: The Immigrant Experience*, Salman Akhtar offered a psychoanalytic approach to

TRAUMA'S DIMENSION WITHIN AND OUTSIDE LANGUAGE

adults' and children's post-migration experiences. He stressed that migrants' ongoing encounters within host cultures lead to an accumulation of inter- and intra-subjective challenges that tax the ego's immediate ability to process the occurrences and adjust. This psychoanalyst and well-published academic claimed that 'no matter how smooth a migrant's transition may be, all international migrations, regardless of circumstances, are perceived by newcomers as a source of trauma' (n.p.).

Newcomers suffer from an immense loss and the need to mourn their past selves and the loved ones left behind. They are affected by the loss of known geographies, familiar foods, music, traditions, and ways of life (Akhtar 1995: 1052–53). Monolingual migrants are also affected by the drastic change in their ability to interact and feel a sense of belonging with dominant groups. Added to such experience is their inability to feel an internal connection with the acquired tongue. Their primary language represents a depth and a sense of wholeness that an acquired tongue cannot duplicate (Carra-Salsberg 2017: 25).

The change in their subject position and inability to feel at home in their surroundings have a disorienting effect on newcomers. During this stage, individuals are caught in the whirlwind of a force that is not symbolized or secured by understanding. Hence, following their relocation, migrants' realities become unintegrated. As seen with many trauma sufferers, to make sense of their realities and heal, many feel the obsessive need to share aspects of their confounding experience(s).

At *Strange Lands*, Akhtar (2012) claimed that the overwhelming nature of the cumulative crises that follow international relocations are experienced and stored at the preconscious level, unlike most traumas. As such, he continued, their experiences are never forgotten (n.p.). In contrast to most traumatic memories, immigrants' recollections of the initial periods in the host country are voluntarily remembered. Yet unlike voluntary everyday recall, such recollections tend to be unaffected by encoding distortions and the passing of time.

Individuals' retrospective longing to testify, reconstruct, and understand the vastness of their remembered crises is seen in published auto-narratives. The need to recall and share is also noted in third-person accounts of migrants' extraordinary lives. Cross-cultural publications often become an admixture of imagined occurrences and vivid, unprocessed replicas of their recalled stressful events. What matters greatly in our discussion is that these empirical narratives

CHILD AND ADOLESCENT MIGRATION, MENTAL HEALTH, AND LANGUAGE

are not studied as facts but as 'systems of meaning and interpretation' that offer instances of individuals' private worlds (Pavlenko 2007: 164–65).

Equally importantly, translingual reconstructions do not only reflect a need to testify to confounding traumas but also reveal migrants' deep-rooted desire to work through their emotions. This is seen in their need to conceptualize the conscious and unconscious guilt that emanates from leaving loved ones behind, surviving, and drastically changing the course of their inner and social lives. This desire to bear witness and justify is also driven by individuals' need to interpret the event(s) that interrupted the linearity of their sense of being. In other words, verbal and written expressions become a mode through which individuals attempt to close the existential gaps that have affected the sense of continuity in their lives (Carra-Salsberg 2017: 12–13, 23).

As argued by Joseph Fernando (2022), with migration and the 'tearing apart of narrative memory', newcomers become exposed to an experience that may resemble that of interpersonal or impersonal traumas. Even if the experience of migration is missing some of trauma's characteristics, such as intrusiveness, as newcomers become immersed within the host/foreign language, the occurrence does involve a breakdown of narrative (n.p.). Yet even when accounting for migration's extraordinary nature and the dislocation and confusion that stem from sudden changes, migrants' trauma, in agreement with Akhtar (2012), becomes preconscious. As such, it becomes central to individuals' need to recall, reconstruct, and understand the chaos of their recalled experiences.

For many newcomers, the preconscious trauma of migration becomes only one component of their harrowing experience. As argued throughout this book, extraordinary events experienced prior to or following individuals' displacement(s), while trying to escape, when partaking in dangerous relocations, and/or when confronted with austere receiving systems and instances of discrimination, become central to the cumulative crises that overwhelm, mark and/or exacerbate the break in a much-needed continuity of experience.

Trauma and Intra-Subjective Splits

When studying testimonies of those who have lived through exceptional circumstances, van der Kolk and van der Hart (1995) highlight individuals' experience of living 'long periods of time in which they live, as it were, in two different worlds: the realm of the trauma and the realm of their current,

TRAUMA'S DIMENSION WITHIN AND OUTSIDE LANGUAGE

ordinary life' (176). When this occurs, their past becomes unreachable, and a future free from trauma becomes perceptually inconceivable (Carra-Salsberg 2017: 26). This duality points to a parallel existence that, for many, becomes 'impossible to bridge' (van der Kolk & van der Hart 1995: 176). As a result, sufferers 'switch from one to the other without synchronization because ... [they are] reporting not a sequence, but a simultaneity' (Langer 1991: 95, cited in van der Kolk & van der Hart 1995: 176–77).

Whether described as distinct, simultaneous occurrences or as a break in temporal reality, the division in experiential realities is a troubling symptom that interferes with one of our universal needs. When addressing our universal condition at the aforementioned conference, Salman Akhtar (2012) claimed that regardless of place of birth, race, ethnicity, language, religion, age, history, and level of education, we all share the same need for love, a sense of belonging, safety, and a sense of temporal continuity. Here we could note that international relocations challenge the latter two, as recently discussed. Aside from the possible affront to individuals' sense of physical and/or emotional safety, migrants experience a disruption in temporal continuity.

We understand that descriptions of trauma are prominent in international migrants' auto-narratives. Not only do those affected by extraordinary traumatic push factors or by traumatizing journeys of international relocation share their accounts of trauma and migration. Those affected by sudden immersions within foreign-host environments also report the rupture in temporal continuity. Often, self-narratives that share recollections of the initial stage of host-/foreign-language immersion highlight how writers felt socially and emotionally overwhelmed by the vastness of their existential change. As seen with phenomenological descriptions of trauma, their break in continuity is marked by a feeling of unreality, disorientation, and a sense of inner chaos. Translingual writers often recall that their pre- and post-migration experiences felt unbridgeable. Along with such a break in subjective continuity, writers commonly describe feeling as though they lived in a never-ending fog during their initial period of relocation (Carra-Salsberg 2017: 23–24).

Newcomers' testimonial experiences lead us to assume that within this current volume, it would be incomplete to focus on child and adolescent migrants and migration's relation to trauma, without paying attention to the psycho-social consequences of host-/foreign-language immersions. Specifically,

CHILD AND ADOLESCENT MIGRATION, MENTAL HEALTH, AND LANGUAGE

it seems apt to explore the link between language, speakers' private and shared realities, and their mental health.

Post-Traumatic Stress Disorder (PTSD) and International Relocations

While many new migrants experience a sense of crisis following their relocation, many struggle to adapt within their new environment because of traumas they experienced prior to their journey. Along such lines, in a 2015 study, McGregor, Melvin, and Newman examined how symptomatologic levels of post-traumatic stress disorder (PTSD) influence minors' sense of belonging, identity formations, relationships, affiliations, and ability to reflect and share their past and current experiences (377). These researchers examined the experiences of high school students who had relocated to Australia for an average of 6.5 years. McGregor et. al divided their participants into two groups depending on their PTSD symptomatology. Results point to how participants with lower PTSD symptomatology had stronger interpersonal bonds, with family members and friends, and with peers from a variety of backgrounds. These participants described having a higher sense of self-worth and a positive connection with their homeland. They also reported experiencing a sense of belonging to and identity with their native country and culture. Furthermore, 'they were self-reflexive and insightful, and most found meaning out of their ... experiences. Their core family units were intact ... family relationships characterized by affection and mutual understanding' (377).

On the other hand, the group of participants characterized by high levels of PTSD symptoms had the tendency to not discuss issues of cultural belongingness to their home or host country. Instead, they stressed feeling a sense of disconnection with both. These participants did not appear to engage reflexively with their past experiences as refugees. Instead, they focused on their present-day concerns. When dealing with stressors, many appeared to use avoidance coping mechanisms. Moreover, this group was characterized by family separations and bitter and conflictual relationships, and expressed that they had difficulties with interpersonal relationships (377–78).

McGregor et al. argue that their results seem to mirror those from previous qualitative studies with resettled refugees. Such studies also stress how youth and adults with low symptom levels of PTSD perceive the importance

TRAUMA'S DIMENSION WITHIN AND OUTSIDE LANGUAGE

of feeling a sense of identification and belongingness to their ethnic communities and homeland. Those with high levels showed a disconnect with both their homeland and the host culture. Adolescents with the positive attitudes towards the host country and ethnic cultures tend to have a higher sense of self-worth and peer acceptance ratings, compared to those with negative attitudes towards the host country and their own ethnic groups (378). When ties and attachments to place are profoundly disrupted, establishing a sense of connection and belongingness is challenging. These researchers suggest that adolescents who are unable to establish a sense of connection and belongingness in the host country and with their own ethnic communities have a higher propensity to develop psychological difficulties. In agreement with this claim, one may suggest that our positive interactions and connections with others offer us a buffer, enabling us to relate, to feel less lonely and better understood—thus making us feel more positive and/or able to embrace our current reality. Sharing our experiences, moreover, may allow us to claim our past, heal, and move forward.

The study also found that "Participants in the low group [of PTSD symptoms] demonstrated a variety of coping and … adaptive cognitive processes (such as their maintenance of strong moral and ideological beliefs) … Optimistic thinking, problem solving, normalization, and ability to consider stressors from others' perspectives … have been found to relate to positive psychological outcomes' (378). McGregor et al. add that 'maintenance of religious and ideological commitments is protective in resettled youth' (378). The same may be said with the maintenance of language. In agreement with McGregor, Melvin, and Newman, it is important for individuals to have 'a coherent narrative and belief system to make sense of their lives' (378). As challenging as it may be for youth who have high levels of PTSD symptomology, for all trauma survivors, sharing and reflecting upon their past and present experiences is part of a process that may lead to healing and an opportunity to move forward.

Conclusion

By drawing from psychoanalytic theory, this chapter has focused on the developmental importance of holding environments during the stages of childhood and adolescence. It highlighted the challenges affecting minors who cross international borders alone or who become separated from their parents while in transit. Likewise, this chapter drew attention to the manner in which

CHILD AND ADOLESCENT MIGRATION, MENTAL HEALTH, AND LANGUAGE

accompanied minors are affected by their primary caregivers' stressors, mental health and/or their inability to support their children's socio-emotional and developmental needs. Central to this chapter is the study of how young migrants' and parents' cumulative stressors or ongoing crises further complicate the challenging stages of childhood and adolescence.

By paying close attention to the relation between migration and mental health, Chapter 4 studied the different types of traumas and their transmissibility. With a focus on international relocations, it stressed how traumas may occur before, during and following their move between countries. It also asserted that regardless of circumstances involving individuals' international relocations and regardless of conditions experienced within transit and/or destination countries, all international migrations and host–foreign language immersions inflict upon newcomers a pre-conscious trauma (n.p.).

The chapter examined the impact of trauma on memory and on minors' short and long-term adjustments. It pointed to how cumulative crises influence minors' short and long-term self–other relations with members from their immediate and extended environments. In addition, it highlighted how impactful occurrences and cumulative crises not only affect individuals' adjustments in the transit and/or host countries, but also influence minors' host-language acquisition and academic performance.

This chapter's focus on childhood, adolescence, trauma, and migration leads us to the study of translingual and cross-cultural auto-narratives and the significance of writing. With a continued attention to the link between language and mental health, chapter five examines how the act of sharing retrospectively constructed, deconstructed, and reconstructed experiences creates a space for understanding, forgiveness, and healing. It looks at how writers often bridge theoretical reflection with the practice of experimental life writing (Karpinski 2012: 17). The following chapter studies how writing testimonials of ordinary and extraordinary occurrences may also be interpreted as a source of qualifying data: shedding light onto the problem of migrancy and its effects on children and adolescents.

5 Bearing Witness to Translingual Realities: A Study of the Significance of First-Person, Cross-Cultural Publications

NEW YORK RAIN is a rain of exile. Abundant, viscous, and dense, it pours down tirelessly between the high cubes of cement into avenues plunged suddenly into the darkness of the well: seeking shelter in a cab that stops at a red light and starts again on a green, you suddenly feel caught in a trap, behind monotonous, fast-moving windshield wipers sweeping aside the water that is constantly renewed. You are convinced you could drive like this for hours without escaping these square prisons or the cisterns through which you wade with no hope of a hill or a real tree. The whitened skyscrapers loom in the grey mist like gigantic tombstones for a city of the dead, and seem to sway slightly on their foundations. At this hour they are deserted. Eight million men, the smell of steel and cement, the madness of builders, and yet the very height of solitude. 'Even if I were to clasp all the people in the world against me, it would protect me from nothing.'

(Camus 1996: 307)

In the essay quoted above, Albert Camus offers his reflections on the existential condition of exile. Through this epigraph, readers are exposed to descriptions of darkness, loneliness, entrapment, destitution, and doom. New York, this metropolis, and home to millions of migrants, is defined as a 'city of the dead', where skyscrapers are like gigantic tombstones and foundations are shaken. He describes himself hopelessly seeking shelter in a cab that is driven by the monotony of traffic and fast-moving windshield wipers. One may assume that his sense of agency is founded on his written expression and the depiction of his grief, loneliness, and inability to connect with the millions of people who surround him.

CHILD AND ADOLESCENT MIGRATION, MENTAL HEALTH, AND LANGUAGE

Even though this existentialist French Algerian writer and philosopher is known for his inclination towards pessimism and absurdism, it is difficult to ignore the relatable truth in his words. Regardless of his partiality to writing about his views on the hopelessness of life, the introduction to his essay meticulously portrays newcomers' initial feelings of displacement, loneliness, and dejection. Through skilful use of literary devices, Camus seems to accurately define the overwhelming anguish many newcomers experience when longing for the sense of home they left behind; when during the initial stages of relocation they feel isolated and unable to emotionally connect with those who form part of their new, and often rejected, physical and social environment.

Cross-Cultural Auto-Narratives as Qualitative Data

To read is to listen, to interpret, and to develop an insight.

(Felman 1987: 23)

As mentioned throughout this book, cross-cultural, first-person narratives are significant objects of disclosure. Such works offer readers a view into writers' past and present translingual realities. In the form of essays, poems, and short and book-length memoirs, translingual writings embody truths reconstructed through the retrospective lens of time. Through their writings, authors are given free rein to disclose intimate details of remembered and sometimes imagined perceptions. Together, these are woven into affective and sociolinguistic stories of love, loss, gains, and transformations. Unlike in interviews, perceptions of events are not elicited, interrupted, or reinterpreted by well-intended researchers. Such narratives are not influenced by academics who may knowingly or unknowingly work with an assumed agenda. Instead, they are composed by writers who hope to 'give their lives meaning across time' (Pavlenko 2007: 164).

Let us bear in mind that, as with all projects, an agenda, whether consciously evident or not, is always present. For translingual writers, their agenda is often founded on a need to conceptualize their memories of displacement. It is also centred on their desire to highlight their lifelong accomplishments in different languages and divergent cultures. Writers' published reconstructions of their experiences may be driven by a need to justify their actions. Translingual expressions are also driven by writers' desire to symbolize.

Along such lines, when examining Lacan's theory of the developmental and authoritative meaning of language, we note that desire and the need to symbolize drive children to use language. Through language, children situate themselves within a structure that moves them beyond the mother–child dichotomy and away from their first love (Felman 1987: 111–12). Not every migrant is driven by a need to write their auto-narratives. Most migrants, however, are affected by the need to tell their own stories: to disclose what their lives used to be like, how hard it was to survive as a migrant, and how far they have come since their change. Here we may suggest a parallel between Lacan's theory and translingual subjects' use of oral and written language: their desire to call, share, and symbolize through retrospective meanings of known and poorly understood experiences that place them within the structure of their new-found world.

Cross-cultural auto-narratives shed light on the socio-cognitive and emotional side of foreign immersions. They provide empirical realities that are offered through writers' intentional disclosures and expose unconscious processes, uprooting unintentional slips of the pen or 'excess in discourse' (Felman 1987: 21). This is founded in the defences that may unknowingly come to light through the process of articulation. As is often seen with translingual narratives, writers' expressions may also bear witness to traces of the guilt that stems from their former need to distance themselves from their first loves and old selves. It stems from their transformations within new languages and realities that may bear little to no trace of their former attachments, conceptualizations, and overall lives.

Language, Gender, and Psychoanalysis: An interpretation of the Other in Translingual Auto-Narratives

Written testimonies from survivors of harrowing occurrences may signify writers' attempts to explain themselves, to bear witness, and possibly to ease confounding emotions of guilt, regret, and/or loss. In this book's previous chapters I have stressed that, when examining the link between language and affect, all verbal, written, and/or signed utterances are products of 1) conscious and unconscious processes, and 2) introjected belief systems that have either been accentuated or canonized by the speaker or writer. When studying translingual or cross-cultural auto-narratives, we note that authors' writings may reflect their known and unknown attempts to symbolize or draw meaning from remembered and seemingly forgotten truths.

From a psychoanalytic vantage point, we understand that Sigmund Freud's theories have focused, for the most part, on boys' ego development within the Oedipal Complex. Such a complex, Freud has argued, is structured within a traditional mother–father binary.[1] According to Lacan, a child's psychosexual relationship also relies of a pre-established social structure. Influenced by Freud (1899, 1910), Lacan asserts that a child's positioning within the social order depends on gender. Yet, as examined by Johnston (2022) when interpreting Lacan's work, for Lacan, the psychical-subjective positions of those involved within the mother–father binary could be 'played by several possible persons of various sex/genders' (n.p.).

A move away from Freud's gender-specific Oedipal relation within a patriarchal social order is seen with Kristeva. In *Revolution of Poetic Language*, Kristeva examines the dynamics that give rise to the ego's development within language. To this effect she argues that within language there is a fluid and plural force that decentres the pre-existing symbolic realm. Kristeva introduces the 'semiotic' as a force that precedes and influences an infant's signifying process (Kristeva 1986: 95). According to Kristeva, during the 'kinetic functional stage' (95), the infant is in a state of symbiosis with their mother's body. This theorist claims that at the earliest stages of life, the child recognizes no distinction between genders. The bisexual fluidity that encompasses the semiotic modality becomes repressed. Such repression, continues Kristeva, occurs through the establishment of the Symbolic Order. Within the symbolic, the child becomes immersed within a realm of positions and identifications. Such immersion, she claims, becomes the threshold of speakers' language (Kristeva 1986: 95, 98).

This play of the semiotic-symbolic and hence non-gendered, bisexual, and/or gender-specific influence is expressed by the subject through their verbal and written expressions. Intersecting with Lacan's view of *lalangue* and language, Kristeva suggests that semiotic repression does not negate its everlasting, veiled influence on the speaking—and writing—subject. The semiotic, she stresses, is a transcendental force that challenges the Symbolic Order (Eagleton 1983: 188). Kristeva suggests that throughout speakers' lives, the semiotic and symbolic become two inseparable modalities within the signifying process (Kristeva 1986: 92–93), which are interdependent aspects of language. According to

Lacan, *lalangue* and the unconscious are accessible through writing (Gutiérrez-Peláez 2015: 145). In a similar vein, Kristeva argues that the semiotic is present within the affective and poetic aspects of language, in speakers' and writers' tone, rhythmical sentences, and images. She suggests that while the semiotic is present within the beauty and rhythm of poetic language, the symbolic exists within its structure: both grammatical and ideological. Yet both the semiotic and symbolic, she continues, interact in the dialogical process of meaning-making and communication.

When addressing the interaction of such forces, Kristeva claims: 'Because the subject is always both semiotic and symbolic, no signifying system that [they produce] can be either exclusively semiotic or exclusively symbolic and is instead marked by the indebtedness of both' (Kristeva 1986: 92–93). In other words, the semiotic, which is 'the Other within language' (Eagleton 1983: 188) or signifier of the unconscious, works alongside the symbolic. The dialectic between them, she continues, 'determines the type of discourse (narrative, metalanguage, theory, or poetry) involved' (Kristeva 1986: 92–93). Influenced by Lacan's and Bakhtinian discourses, Kristeva sees the emergence of a child's subjectivity through the use and discursive understanding of language, which includes the interpretation and accentuation of signs. As with Lacan, Kristeva conceptualizes a primary symbolic code of meanings as a constituent part of the ego's formation. She understands language as born from an inner and social force that aids in the development of speakers' subjectivity—one that splits the subject, while allowing them to identify, relate to the Other, and make sense of the discursive, conscious-unconscious complexity that surrounds them.

The Significance of Writing

One aspect of trauma that matters greatly to this book's overall discussion is the fact that its effects on both adults and children may improve and even dissipate when individuals articulate their occurrence(s) through speech (Caruth 1995: 154; van der Kolk & van der Hart 1995: 176). As argued in *Trauma: Explorations in memory*, when a traumatic event becomes synthesized and integrated through language, sufferers may decode their trauma and incorporate parts of the event into a narrative of the past (Caruth 1995: 153). even when not precise, sharing their recalled experiences or truths through secondary processes grants individuals the opportunity to move forward, close their

CHILD AND ADOLESCENT MIGRATION, MENTAL HEALTH, AND LANGUAGE

temporal and existential gap, and potentially understand the symptoms that, until then, posed a confounding intrusion in their lives.

Along such lines, in *Retelling the Stories of Our Lives*, David Denborough (2014) discusses the healing capacity of narrative therapy. He focuses on the importance of writing letters and even visual illustrations, charts, or lists for imagined and/or actual audiences. He stresses the transformative quality of written expressions and how they often alter and/or afford a sense of clarity to the manner in which individuals construe their socio-affective experiences. Written expressions, continues Denborough, influence how individuals see themselves, how they interpret their past and the continuum of their realities (4). He suggests that this alternative form of psychotherapy empowers writers: it allows individuals to break from the isolating nature of loss, trauma, and/or mental illness (121). By giving voice to their past, individuals externalize the confounding events that impede their ability to move forward (121). By drawing attention to significant setbacks, writers facilitate change and reclaim their lives (141–42). Equally importantly, disclosing selective aspects of their lives shapes writers' sense of who they are and who they wish to become.

Denborough's words parallel those of the linguist Aneta Pavlenko (2007), who, while analysing published self-narratives, argues that writers use language to symbolize and interpret their worlds, position themselves as subjects, and give their lives meaning across time (164). Even though Pavlenko refers to published self-narratives, while Denborough discusses the effects of writing unpublished work, such as personal letters and charts, we may agree that writing to actual or imagined audiences influences subjects' (re)interpretation of their past and present realities. Writing often allows writers to feel understood, and this, in turn, allows for them to close the existential gap that has affected their lives. Moreover, the crucial act of piecing together dislocated events that have affected our lives allows for a needed sense of temporal continuity through time (Akhtar 1995: 1066).

Trauma, Language, and the Remaking of the Self

When exposed to the violence and shock of a horrifying trauma, finding words to share an indescribable experience may seem impossible, at least initially. In *The Girl Who Smiled Beads: A Story of War and What Comes After*, Clementine Wamariya (2018) mentions such inability. Wamariya describes how, as a

BEARING WITNESS TO TRANSLINGUAL REALITIES

six-year-old survivor of the Rwanda Massacre, at night after walking for hours with Claire, her older sister, lost and confused, Wamariya heard laughing, screaming, pleading, and crying:

> I didn't know how to name the noises. They were human and non-human. I never learned the right words in Kinyarwanda. I hope they don't exist. But without words, my mind had no way to define or understand the awful sounds, nowhere to store them in my brain. (25)

Here we read how Wamariya's experience, since it did not fit any pre-existing schema, became untranslatable. As is the case with traumas, it become unprocessed, suspended in what Joseph Fernando (2018) calls 'a zero-process' (40). Wamariya was thus unable to register or store her memory using language. Moreover, since her confounding experience took place at night while she and her sister were hiding, the significant event was devoid of images. Thus, it was not stored as an iconic memory either. Instead, it became stored in the form of emotions. As discussed later in her memoir, only by sharing through her writing was she able 'to find a way to tolerate the intolerable truth' (233) of her extraordinary experiences as a trauma survivor over time.

Unfortunately, experiences of childhood trauma are read too often in cross-cultural narratives written by former refugee children and youth. In this book's first chapter, we discussed Uwiringiyimana's experiences of racial divide and persecution when she and her family barely escaped the violence of an angry crowd (Uwiringiyimana 2017: 68–73). It seems fitting to mention that added to their displacement, the occurrence that amounted to this writer's 'meaning of her obsessive act' involved a nightly ambush that took place in 2003 after she and her family settled in a makeshift camp:

> The killers who attacked our camp were rebels from Burundi, and they did not want us there. We were outsiders again. On that night, I thought my life was over. My mother and sister had been gunned down. I had blacked out from fear, then tried to flee, only to find a gun pointed at my head … it was all beyond my control. Then, in a flash amid the chaos, somehow I got kicked to the ground. The gunman went chasing after someone else … I got up and fled. I stumbled, I fell, I ran. Around me people were burning, crying in pain, dying … I just ran … I made it to a nearby farm … A woman was there, and I tensed up. I didn't know if she was one of my people … She took me by the hand and we wandered … [past] the haunted faces of survivors … [After being

told by her uncle that her mother was dead] … like an image from a dream, Mom appeared before me … We hugged each other hard … She was bleeding, shivering in pain … And then a realization swept through my body … My mother was not with Deborah. My little sister had been clinging on my mom during the attack, never leaving her side … Deborah died in the clothes she wore to bed that night, including my hand-me-down soccer jersey that she loved … Now she would never wear my clothes again. She would not grow up with me … Deborah had been shot in the head, but she survived long enough to say the heartbreaking words to my mom, 'Hold me'. (74–78)

Uwiringiyimana's need to share her truth in writing points to an inner need to establish a linearity within her life and 'remember' (242), to understand her nightmares and 'shattering images flooding back from the massacre' (235).

Her ability to speak about the past and reconstruct her experiences took time. Like many survivors of a shared trauma, Uwiringiyimana's family had no common language to describe their experiences and avoided reopening the wounds and re-experiencing the weight of their upsetting past (237). Over time, Uwiringiyimana was able to reconstruct her lived occurrences, work through her trauma, and better understand her complex reality as a survivor. Through photo exhibits depicting images of those who lived through the Gatumba Massacre, along with her involvement in the Women in the World Summit, and eventually her writing, Uwiringiyimana came to terms with her past and present life.

For Uwiringiyimana, following her years of anger and moments of depression, sharing and conceptualizing her history created a space for healing. By educating others and turning passivity into activity, she drew attention to the realities that affected and continue to affect populations worldwide (196). As with many writers, sharing her reconstructed memories allowed Uwiringiyimana to reclaim her past and integrate her trauma into her schemata and framework of experiences. In her terms, retelling her story allowed her to sort her feelings, move forward, grieve her past self, honour her sister's memory, and begin to feel a sense of hope for her future (250).

Testifying to a Life between Languages

The exiled writer is someone who has left the cage of an oppressive political system; but if he is to remain a writer at all, he must never really leave another cage—that of his native language. There, he is gagged; here, he is

BEARING WITNESS TO TRANSLINGUAL REALITIES

tongue-tied. The ultimate irony: those who are the most tongue-tied may have the most to say.

(Baranczak 1996: 251)

In *Switching Languages*, Stephen Kellman (2003) highlights the connection between language and affect. By studying translingual writers' descriptions of language-related experiences of migrancy,[2] Kellman focuses on the link between foreign-language immersion and newcomers' psychology—specifically, migrants' ability to transform within grounds that, at least initially, make monolingual migrants feel othered. Kellman presents the case of Czesław Miłosz, a Polish poet who moved to the United States at the age of forty-nine and, after living in California for over fifty years, chose to write poetry and prose in his mother tongue. In his memoir, Milosz openly rationalizes the root of his refusal to use English, his second language, when he states:

In my rejection of imposing a profound change on myself by going over to writing in a different language, I perceive a fear of losing my identity, because it is certain that when we switch languages, we become someone else. (Cited in Kellman 2003: xiv)

For this writer, his resistance to switching languages is tied to his need to honour and uphold the mother language that is associated with his memory of wholeness and unquestioned identity. Understanding the link between language, identity, memory, and affect gives us insight into why many adolescent and adult migrants are unwilling or simply unable to fully introject a second tongue. While focusing on individuals' perceived inability to switch and fully identify themselves with a foreign language, David Block (2007) explains that age and ego development play an enormous role in individuals' ego permeability. Since minors' ego boundaries are developmentally fluid, children are able to introject the new language and eventually internalize it as their own. On the other hand, adults have established ego boundaries and hence feel increasingly challenged by the internalization of a new linguistic code (51–52). Block's claim may be linked to that of Akhtar (2012), who, at a psychoanalytic conference in Toronto,[3] explained that when individuals migrate as adults, since their ego boundaries have been—for the most part—solidified, subjects are less likely to undertake drastic linguistic changes.

CHILD AND ADOLESCENT MIGRATION, MENTAL HEALTH, AND LANGUAGE

It also seems appropriate to suggest that for many migrants, the inability to translate themselves and thus switch internal languages also relates to their emotional attachment to their mother tongue. The affective significance of a first language is not new to anyone who has experienced linguistic shifts. It is therefore a common theme among writers who describe their experiences within and between tongues. If we look closely at Marjorie Agosín's writing, we can see that in her memoir 'Words: a basket of love', Agosín openly supports the emotional meaning of her primary language when she testifies:

> Language defined my past ... I never stopped writing in Spanish because I could not abandon my essence, the fragile, divine core of my being. It would have meant becoming someone else, frequenting sadness, losing my soul and all the butterflies. I always spoke Spanish. Even in my solemn dreams. I did not want to translate myself. (2003: 324)

Agosín migrated to the United States from Chile when she was nineteen years old and acquired a high level of bilingualism during her years living in the USA. Still, the Spanish language remains her creative tongue. Like Milosz, Agosín perceived her primary language as the only language that defines her history, rendering the Spanish language the only suitable medium of emotions.

At this point in our discussion, it is necessary to highlight that remaining true to one's first language in the face of socio-geographic change is not embraced by all migrants, willingly or unwillingly. Many individuals migrate as young adults, and due to financial obligations and social needs, they acquire and eventually master a host language. With such individuals, explains Lambert, the foreign-host linguistic code becomes something more than a reference group and a reference language. Their linguistic shift affects not only their linguistic comfort within the acquired tongue, but also their relationship with their primary symbolic code. For Lambert, 'the more proficient a person becomes in a second language, the more [they] may find that [their] place in [their] original membership group is modified'. As a result, explains this linguist, the subject may 'experience feelings of chagrin or regret as [they lose] ties with [their original] group' (cited in Block 2007: 48). Lambert argues that the feelings linked to language learners' sudden change in linguistic and social behaviour are annexed to the concept of anomie, which, according to Block, is defined by experiences of internal conflict and feelings of 'moral chaos' (48–50). In other words, switching languages may result in the guilt that stems from

BEARING WITNESS TO TRANSLINGUAL REALITIES

replacing the language that became unconsciously linked to our first object(s) of affection (Carra-Salsberg 2015b: 32).

Similarly, Eva Karpinski (2012) suggests that the giving up of a primary language's instrumental function involves becoming transformed or remade within the flow of the foreign other (1–2). This loss, she argues, concerns linguistic displacements that relate to individuals' dislocation within language and within the self (3). Karpinski stresses the radical change in subjectivity when translating, or attempting to translate, oneself within a host language, which involves a disorienting conscious and/or unconscious crisis that rises from a primary language's significance within the development and under-standing of the subject's inner being and subjective core.

The Subject in Crisis: Navigating through the Vicissitudes of Young Migrants' Foreign-Host Sociolinguistic Transformations

Being a new migrant implies living through the crisis that stems from the loss of their former selves, former socio-affective connections, familiar landscapes, ways of life, and sense of home (Akhtar 1995: 1052). When individuals— willingly or unwillingly—leave their homeland and become transplanted into a new world, they experience the crisis that rises from the gap between their present and their past. As seen with most traumatic experiences, individuals become fixed within a never-ending present in which their past is inaccessible, and a view of an enjoyable future within their newly imposed reality seems impossible. Newcomers, young and old, are overcome by their loss in experi-ential continuity and the stress resulting from comparing their confounding present with a highly idealized past.

Such constant comparison and its effect on newcomers' inability to move on are common themes in translingual memoirs, especially those that describe newcomers' initial stages of host-cultural adjustment. Returning to *How Dare the Sun Rise*, Sandra Uwiringiyimana (2017) describes such challenges when she narrates:

> The houses on our street were all very close together, but none of our neigh-bors came over and introduced themselves.
>
> No one knocked on our door. Mom was surprised at how lonely and iso-lated America felt. The neighbors didn't seem to know each other. People

locked their doors. Everyone kept to themselves. Mom would look out the window and ask, 'Where are all the people?'

Back home on our sunny, friendly street in Uvira, we had people coming and going in our house all the time. People smiled and said hello when they passed you on the street. We never locked doors. (123–24)

Newcomers' past experiences become a central point of reference through which the unintegrated nature of their present is measured. As highlighted by Akhtar (1995), newcomers grieve their missed experiences, familiar landscapes, and expectable behaviours (1052). New migrants also grieve the sense of familiarity and socio-emotive connectivity they experienced with those who formed part of their immediate environment and extended reality.

The difficulty in communicating and the differences marked in people's ways of life are not the only barriers newcomers experience when immersed within a foreign linguistic and sociocultural reality. As argued in Chapter 1, belief systems also highlight newcomers' peripheral existence or sense of otherness and non-integration with members of the host community. Within their new-found reality, the language of their emotional make-up becomes an inadequate form of expression. In addition, their attempts at translating themselves within a foreign tongue add to the subjective disorientation that estranges them from their known life.

While adults may maintain significant aspects of their cultural identity and, thus, a 'sense of inner continuity in change' (Akhtar 1995: 1056), young migrants are affected by the clash between pre- and post-migration introjections. Young individuals who migrate with members of their immediate family are affected by the tension between their caregivers' traditions and their own developmental need to change. While attempting to negotiate a new sociocultural and linguistic reality, child and adolescent migrants feel caught in a conflict between their caregivers' wish for continuity in behaviours and traditions, and minors' drive to adjust within and conform to their new environment. For children and adolescents, the influential force of dialogic interactions with members of the host community implies an eventual distancing from their past selves and ways of interpreting the complexity of their worlds. Such influence, in turn, affects the manner in which they view their reality and see themselves.

The crisis that evolves through their sudden change in reality and, consequently, their identity is fostered by the young individual's 'internal dialogues'

BEARING WITNESS TO TRANSLINGUAL REALITIES

with themselves. Joseph Sandler and Anne-Marie Sandler (1998) claim that during the period of childhood and adolescence, young individuals 'constantly and automatically' examine their self-image to reassure themselves that there is no gap between the old and current self. When individuals perceive the difference between the old and new self, they can become highly anxious and even panic (97–98, cited in Akhtar 2009: 80). Even though life changes are indisputably natural in all stages of life, during the initial stages of foreign immersion, newcomers encounter challenges related to the suddenness in their experiential change. At the initial stages of foreign immersion, young migrants' subjective transformation is radical and, as such, highly disorienting. The anxiety evoked by this confounding experience is further heightened by the shock derived from their internal dialogue.

The experience of becoming distanced from a former life is described in Uwiringiyimana's memoir. Once fluent in English and influenced by dialogic encounters within her host environment, Uwiringiyimana experienced a disconnection from her former self. By way of displacement, this writer also felt a divide from her parents. While adults' ego boundaries are set and thus less open to sudden conceptual changes, Uwiringiyimana's subjective transformation increased her level of separation from her first love objects. When attempting to negotiate her new reality, Uwiringiyimana felt unable to share her concerns with her mother and father. In addition to her unwillingness to add to her parents' stress, Uwiringiyimana felt that her parents would not understand the social and school-related challenges she was experiencing or the changes she was undergoing through her process of assimilation:

> I was taking steps, but they [my parents] were taking leaps ... they had their traditions and values, and I was growing up in a different world, a different culture. I had to try not to get too far ahead of them, and they had to try to catch up with me ... Parents have to learn how to raise their children in a foreign land. Kids need guidance from their parents, but their parents have no idea what influences their children are facing in their new world. (182)

For Uwiringiyimana, the inner estrangement caused by her attempt to adjust and the resulting strain that existed between herself and her parents created a relational displacement, from her parents to Pastor Linda.[4] In her memoir, Uwiringiyimana describes how this pastor became a new influential

CHILD AND ADOLESCENT MIGRATION, MENTAL HEALTH, AND LANGUAGE

figure in her American life, filling the void left by her parents' latest inability to guide their teenage children:

> Pastor Linda, a white woman, quickly became one of my favorite people ... My parents were having a difficult time parenting in America because they didn't know the language or the culture. I began asking Linda things I would ordinarily ask them, like about words or phrases I had heard people use. Her kids were grown, and she spent a lot of time with my siblings and me, answering questions, helping us with homework, offering advice. She was a calming voice ... her guidance and faith were soothing to me ... [I began to rethink] what God meant to me personally. I had been angry at him, but I decided to give him another chance. (136–38)

Added to the ideational and relational dissonance, Uwiringiyimana's incipient rejection of her parents' values may also be read as an augmentation of her second individuation. Adolescents' individuation is part of a natural developmental process that, through the eventual distancing and independence from the parents, leads to the individual's subjective growth. This period entails the fusion of drives, the organization of the ego, and the development of a superego (Akhtar 1995: 1053). It involves the introjection of society's ideals and sense of morals. While highly influenced by the dominant culture, young migrants' second individuation and distancing often extend to their caregivers' values, traditions, and overall conceptualizations. Consistent with Akhtar, individuation involves a positive move towards growth and independence. This can be challenging to parents as it sometimes affects minors' interpretation of their parents' authority.

Uwiringiyimana describes her double life as a young migrant who felt distanced from her parents:

> I hated the fact that I couldn't be a normal kid, like the kids around me, their parents were in charge, and they understood how things worked ... I was leading a double life, trying to be an American kid at school but coming home to teach my parents English and help them pay the bills. Kids aren't supposed to teach their parents ... everything my parents knew from American culture came from me. But I still knew so little myself. (174)

Another significant challenge linked to young migrants' condition as newcomers involves the experience of inner and outwardly expressed anger. The sources of anger may vary. Some might be linked to their stage of development and/or home dynamics. For migrants, however, their anger may also be linked to the disillusionment and resentment that stem from role reversals. Accompanied young migrants become aware of their parents' vulnerabilities and struggles within the host environment. While some children feel the need to become protected by their parents, others may resent the cessation of their sense of protection (Salsberg 2017: 21). As children navigate the universal waters of development and change, instead of relying on their parents' protection and guidance, they feel unsheltered. Moreover, their parents' attempts to guide their children may be perceived as inept in contending with the realities of their host sociocultural environment.

Examining Adults' Influence on Children

Judith Ortiz Cofer (2015) portrayed the affective underpinnings of a mother tongue and migrants' sense of loss and grief in her autobiography, *The Cruel Country*. Following her mother's death, this Puerto Rican writer reminisces about her past as a young, recurrent migrant. However, for most of her life, she grew up in the United States with her brother, mother, and father. Her father worked in the military, and hence was regularly stationed away from home. Throughout her book, she recounts her experiences in both countries, Puerto Rico and the United States. One of the most prominent aspects of her constructed truths reflects the memories of her parents' inability to adjust to their lives in the United States, their host country. Ortiz Cofer describes their long-lasting homesickness and the manner in which such sadness affected her as a child. She states:

> Homesickness is called a sickness for a reason. It can be either brief or chronic, and when it becomes part of someone's life, as it must have for my mother and perhaps my father, it turns into what has been labeled by sociologists as cultural grief or bereavement ... that is a sense of loss that does not abate. I am trying to understand what my parents must have felt when they left their culture as young people, and found a list of symptoms and behaviours familiar from our early lives on the mainland [United States] ... Grief over the loss of family and friends, over the loss of the mother tongue, over the loss of culture; grief over the loss of the homeland, over the loss of contact with your ethnic group, over the fear of physical danger; grief over the loss of the original dream and the grief of no possible return (171–72).

CHILD AND ADOLESCENT MIGRATION, MENTAL HEALTH, AND LANGUAGE

Ortiz Cofer continues with the description of her mother's deep sorrow, stating that 'her grief was not complicated; hers was simple grief over temporary dislocation. She was irritated by her inability to express herself. She yearned for family and friends … she feared being sick and being unable to get help for one of us if we fell ill' (172); returning home to Puerto Rico was always her plan. Through her writing, Ortiz Cofer allows her readers to note the way in which migrating and having one's sense of self deconstructed impacts us. Equally importantly, she also offers us a glimpse into how parents' realities, situations, and feelings, which we may not be able to fully grasp or control, affect us deeply.

When reading cross-cultural auto-narratives of writers' past experiences of culture shock, depression and dislocations or intra-subjective splits are, unfortunately, common. Returning to *Cruel Country*, Ortiz Cofer not only shares her mother's loneliness and grief, but also narrates her father's depression and his 'accidents', both of which the author describes as seemingly intentional:

> The greatest prueba [test] in our lives was my father's illness … I remember my father's first major breakdown and how both she and I fought against the reality of what it meant. He was in such despair that he wanted to die … One evening during my first year of college, I came home to a frantic phone call from my mother telling me that my father had fallen from a building and had been hospitalized with almost every bone in his body broken. (78)

While he survived his first accident, his second accident, 'involving a head-on collision between [her] father's Volkswagen and an embarkment wall' (88), was fatal. As with most children, regardless of age, following her father's death, she was overcome by guilt:

> I believe now that I was in denial out of guilt for not giving my father my full attention while he lived, for not responding when he said, after I showed my parents my first published poems, 'Maybe you can write my story.' I did not want to know his story. His story frightened me. I was afraid I would end up like him, already having experienced my own dark days and nights of inexplicable sadness by then. (89)

We understand that depression is not limited to newcomers. We also know that Ortiz Cofer's father had been in the military, and his sadness may be related to a traumatic encounter he had while deployed. However, one may

BEARING WITNESS TO TRANSLINGUAL REALITIES

suppose that being a migrant adds to individuals' pre-existing challenges or predispositions to become or remain depressed.

An equally noteworthy aspect of *The Cruel Country* rests in Ortiz Cofer's description of the moment she fell in love with the English language, realizing that the literature opened doors to new worlds and the power of language:

> It was at St. Joe's that I began my long romance with language, and I owe it to one nun that broke my mold, who saw my word-hunger and fed it. With her I learned that I would never have to be lonely again ... I began to focus on one area I knew would save me from the bubble: literature. I learned that language, specifically the English language, was my medium ... Later I would memorialize my first mentor in an essay as 'Sister Rosetta.' And she was my Rosetta Stone, teaching me to decipher the foreign tongue, showing me how to assert my dominance over the language that I needed to make mine by giving me books to read ... feeding my hungry mind. By helping me not be invisible and silent, she helped me change my *destino* forever. I became a book addict then, consuming words without restraint. Never again hungry for words. (69–70)

Ortiz Cofer's need to create her path through knowledge and host-language dominance may be seen as a way to break from parents' existential realities. This need to introject and make language and aspects of the host culture one's own is often read in translingual memoirs. Ortiz Cofer's words and relation between learning destruction and recreation is a reverberation of Pitt's (2006) link between significant language learning and matricide, as discussed in Chapter 3. .

Language, Writing, and Transformation

While a mother tongue is linked to a speaker's history of affect and first love objects, for children and adolescent migrants, a host language may signify a need to individuate, transform, synthesize, and even break from the oppressiveness and traumas that represent their past. As the language often linked to their education, a host language is also the medium of writing and expression. Thus, it is often the language through which writers conceptualize their experiences, understand their past, and heal.

This search for understanding through self-expression is depicted by Ha-yun Jung (2004) in 'Personal and singular'. In her brief auto-narrative, Jung

CHILD AND ADOLESCENT MIGRATION, MENTAL HEALTH, AND LANGUAGE

walks her readers through two significant migrations and life between regions, schools, social circles, and languages. As a child and adolescent, this writer travelled from Seoul, Korea to Bangkok, Thailand and back to Seoul. We learn how her experiences within countries changed from being the daughter and granddaughter of prestigious, well-respected diplomats, to losing such prestige and wealth. Along with such upheavals came the consequences of her father's poor health, the progression of her mother's changeable psycho-emotional state, her eventual suicide, and later, her brother's death.

Her writing begins with a distinction in address between Korean and English, stating that in Korean, 'the first-person singular is an elusive voice', as the 'I' is typically replaced by the third-person plural. She then claims that 'Rarely will you hear a Korean speak—or write—consecutive sentences that start with this I-that, I-that. "I" seems content to crawl behind the curtain at the first given moment.' The same occurs with possessive pronouns: 'our' is often used in place of 'my' (165).

Even though at first glance, Jung's remarks on the difference in use of subject pronouns are linked to a distinction between cultures, throughout her narrative, it becomes evident that her focus on such differences is also linked to the personal feelings she attached to each of her internalized languages.

This narrative offers a glimpse into the writer's memories of socio-emotional dislocations, subjective shifts, and loss. Jung's recalled sense of location and dislocation are linked to the countries in which her subjective shifts took place, and the language through which she communicated and conceptualized her reality.

As previously discussed in this book, our language becomes consciously and unconsciously linked to our earliest experiences. For many of us, our first language is linked to the feeling of being cared for, protected, and loved by our primary caregivers. Through the law of relationality, the emotions we feel towards our first language are linked to the love we experienced as infants.

Interconnected with this volume's earlier discussions of Winnicott's work and the link between language and our history of affect, in 'About losing and being lost', Anna Freud (1967 [1958]) highlights the symbolic link between individuals' specific material possessions and individuals' love objects. With such association, possessions become libidinally cathected and objects' cathexis increases, decreases, or changes from positive to negative or from libido to aggression depending on the feelings individuals have towards the object in

108

BEARING WITNESS TO TRANSLINGUAL REALITIES

the external world (99). We have established throughout this book that our mother tongue is emotionally linked to our primary love objects and earliest beginnings. Hence, the language we share or used to share with our caregivers becomes libidinally cathected with the positive and/or negative emotions and experiences associated with our first loves.

For Jung, even though her earliest experiences and memories of love are linked to her first language, such language is also tainted with the experiences that involved her return to Seoul: her family's fall from social grace as well as the deaths of her parents and brother. For this writer, the affect imprinted in the Korean language is juxtaposed with the feelings that stemmed from her sense of tragedy and loss. English, on the other hand, became the language of writing: one of conceptualizations, and retrospective understanding. It became associated with migration and Jung's eventual break from the sorrows and despair she experienced in Seoul. As a medium of self-expression, this second language became part of a process through which she was able to heal and grasp her transformational reality as a translingual writer:

> I started to keep a diary in English ... it had become a language that was completely personal and singular to me. Recently, I dug out the old, yellowed notebook from a box that I have carried with me across states and countries and continents ... my writing was entirely devoid of descriptions and details, with hardly a mention of friends or family, filled with sentences that began with 'I' ... words were coming from solely within myself, a place disconnected with the outside world, a place where no one or nothing else could find a way in. (159–60)

English became an adopted language of self-discovery, and yet a language of limited comfort. The author describes being stuck between English, the language of forgetting, and Korean, the language linked to her history of affect. Such in-betweenness is read when she states: 'And I live on, not feeling whole in Korean or in English. For me, one language is complimentary to the other, one always lacking a capacity that the other has. And I have a fear, constantly, of not being quite understood in just one language' (160). This writer's trauma within language creates a split in her life. Her spoken languages, instead of offering a sense of continuity through time, places, and experiences, provide her with a sense of outsideness and incompleteness. Her feelings of love and loss are embedded in both her Korean and English speech. Love and loss

CHILD AND ADOLESCENT MIGRATION, MENTAL HEALTH, AND LANGUAGE

are also seen through her English writing, which encompasses her search for understanding and inability to feel whole.

The theme of linguistic lacerations, dislocations, and a sense of in-betweenness in relation to histories, places, and languages is also evident in Louis Begley's (2005) 'On being an orphaned writer'. As this writer narrates his early experiences between languages, we learn that for Begley, English, which is not his first or even second language (162), becomes his mode of expression as a novelist. After describing the manner in which the experiences of his characters resemble his own (163, 170), Begley highlights that his novels' themes are greatly 'human themes ... not limited by national, religious or ... social boundaries'. Accordingly, such themes involve 'the effect on us of losing those we love the most; our profound and total loneliness, from which only the power of Eros liberates us; the randomness of the catastrophes that befall us; and the hash we make of relationships that count for us the most' (170). For readers, it seems commonsensical to connect such 'universal' themes with concerns expressed by migrants torn between their primary and later languages.

Love, loss, loneliness, melancholia, guilt, and a sense of inner crises—or sense of inner catastrophes—are classic themes in auto-narratives, especially in the works of adults looking back at their child and adolescent experiences of pre- and post-international migrancy.

Anna Freud's theory on displacement of affect supports our earlier claim. It draws attention to the affective significance of a mother tongue and the feelings young migrants often experience when a later language is acquired. It is not uncommon for language learners to describe a sense of guilt that rises when a host language is learned and internalized. This feeling relates to the loss experienced when, out of necessity, the host language becomes the dominant language of expression. The social demotion or partial loss in social meaning of a mother tongue is equivalent to the guilt individuals often experience when an object of emotional importance becomes lost. In her chapter 'About Losing and Being Loss', Anna Freud (2015) states:

> We feel unhappy, miserable, and therefore *deprived*—castration distress— after losing an object. This is because of its subjective value as representative of ... the important love object ... We go through a period of detaching from it as we do when *mourning* a dead person. We also feel *guilty* as if we lost the thing intentionally—as a fully conscious act. (102, italics in original)

BEARING WITNESS TO TRANSLINGUAL REALITIES

In addition, and as previously highlighted in this book, the feelings of nostalgia migrants often experience when they hear their first language spoken may be linked to buried memories of their earliest beginnings. Once again, our first language is unconsciously bound to the earliest feelings we experienced when our ego was yet to be structured. We unknowingly yearn for our former feelings of omnipotence, as argued by Winnicott, and, returning to Lacan, of being whole instead of being divided between the known and the unknown, or the conscious and unconscious realities that form part of our existence as split subjects.

Migration and Child–Parent Estrangements

While matricide is part of a normal and healthy transition towards independence, we note that migrants' child–parent estrangement often becomes heightened, when compared with non-migrants. In *The Girl Who Smiled Beads: A Story of War and What Comes After*, Clemantine Wamariya (2018) narrates her story of love, war, and loss. Her memoir begins in 2006 with an invitation to the Oprah show. At the time, Wamariya was an eighteen-year-old high school student who had entered an essay contest. With her older sister, Claire, she drove to downtown Chicago, expecting to discuss her reading of Elie Wiesel's memoir, *Night*, and its parallels with her childhood experiences as a survivor of the Rwanda Massacre. When called on stage, however, she was surprised to learn that Oprah intended to reunite her and her sister with her family:

> a door that had images of barbed wire on it … opened … and out came an eight-year-old-boy, who was apparently my brother. He was followed by my father, in a dark suit … and a shiny new five-year-old-sister; my mother in a long blue dress; and my sister Claudette, now taller than me … I'd fantasized about this moment so many times … my knees gave out … The cameras were so far away that I forgot I was participating in a million-viewer spectacle, that my experience, my joy and pain, were being consumed by the masses. (6–7)

Wamariya's memoir takes readers through her happy childhood and life after being separated from her family. She tells her readers that together with Claire, her older sister, she was forced to flee in hopes of eventually reuniting with their family. The two young sisters became displaced within Africa, moving from one refugee camp to the next. They experienced violence, poverty, and despair. Their extensive strife shaped their lives, their emotional attachments, and their

CHILD AND ADOLESCENT MIGRATION, MENTAL HEALTH, AND LANGUAGE

lifelong views of the world. When describing her sense of homelessness and yearning for protection at six years of age, Wamariya states:

> I imagined my mother or my father or my grandmother coming. I cried until I couldn't cry anymore. I only knew lives like this existed in stories—lives without mattresses, lives with rats. I was ready to be found, ready to go, not to live like this ...
>
> It's strange how you go from being a person who is away from home to a person with no home at all. The place that is supposed to want you has pushed you out. No other place takes you in. You are unwanted, by everyone. You are a refugee. (29)

Her disconnection with her parents and her emotionally distanced sister during her developmental years affected her ability to establish long-lasting connections. Following her parents' return to her life, she envied her younger siblings' closeness with them—how their uninterrupted love differed from her own experiences:

> They [her parents] stopped talking whenever Claire and I walked into the room. Perhaps this was inevitable—that we would become permanent aliens, irreparably estranged ... I'd see my youngest sister, who was six, jump into my mother's lap. She'd beg for my mother's attention, like all lucky little girls do. (144)

During her foundational years, Wamariya was not exposed to the love and security of a nurturing environment. Instead, she experienced absence and stress. Her older sister looked after her, but she was too busy trying to survive financially while caring for her young children to offer a sense of hope in despair.

When describing her school experience a year following her relocation, when she was thirteen years of age, Wamariya writes: 'I wasn't like the teenagers in my school. My mother and father were ... who? Nobody in my life attended parent–teacher conferences. Nobody made doctor appointments for me. Nobody checked to see if I did my homework' (53). Still, at age thirteen, Wamariya moved to Mrs Thomas's home during weekdays.[5] While living with her 'new American mother' (54), Wamariya felt initially immune to the attention she was receiving from Mrs Thomas and her friends:

> Around Kenilworth, people wanted to treat me like an egg, the poor fragile refugee girl. They said, with the best intentions, 'Let's do something

special for you. Let's buy you something nice.' I was contemptuous and cold. My attitude was, *Okay, if that makes you feel better. If that's your way of giving, if it makes you sleep at night—yes, let's do something nice for me, fine.* (58)

When describing her shopping experience with Mrs Thomas's friend, she later says:

I did not fully understand her project at the time. I did not know how much I was broadcasting my pain, how obvious it was that I needed help loving myself ... The truth is, I needed ... the confidence and positivity she wanted to instil in me. (60)

To grasp Wamariya's response and relation to her parental absence, we should consider Winnicott's (2005) theory of the transitional phenomenon and the significance of being raised in a 'good enough' environment. In *Playing and Reality*, Winnicott offers the definition of a transitional object as one that helps subjects' necessary transition from dependence to independence. He stresses that such an object could only become developmentally relevant to the child when the internal object—the magically introjected breast—is alive, real, and not persecutory (13, 19), after the 'good enough mother' provides her infant with enough opportunity for illusion and, later, gradual disillusionment (15–17). This child psychoanalyst explains that if the external object's, the primary caregiver's, efforts do not meet the needs of the infant, then the internal object fails to have meaning, a situation that results in the meaninglessness of the transitional object as well (13).

Winnicott's theory discloses the difficulty perceived by subjects who experienced a sense of emotional discontinuity during their foundational stages of development. It speaks of the challenges undergone by those who have been raised by primary caregivers who, for a number of possible reasons, were unable to provide an environment that nourished their child's healthy developmental growth. Winnicott supports his theory by describing, in more detail, the case of a woman who, as a child, was separated from her mother for extensive periods of time. According to Winnicott, what affected this patient throughout her young and adult life was the feeling of internal disconnection that developed from her mother's absence. Eventually, this patient felt that the only thing real was the consistency of her nostalgia, the ongoing sense of absence or amnesia (30–32).

CHILD AND ADOLESCENT MIGRATION, MENTAL HEALTH, AND LANGUAGE

The long-term implications of experiencing caregivers' absence include the development of an unintegrated personality. Such developmental deviation, continues Winnicott, inevitably trickles into the subjects' self–other relations (89–90) and correspondingly, into their interactions within their third space.[6] Even though Winnicott's developmental theory is grounded on infantile events, one may argue that his focus on the importance of maintaining a nurturing and stable environment is nevertheless applicable to childhood experiences. Unfortunately, Wamariya's experience is not unique within the realm of migration. Many other unaccompanied minors and refugee children orphaned by violence and wars are equally affected by the cessation of their caregiver's presence and of the sense of safety and uninterrupted love that are necessary for their healthy development.

Conclusion

> say a bird hits this window right here. You and I, we're strangers ... We've come to this moment from different places. I might be terrified of the smash and the carnage, recoil as if the bird were a bomb. You might think I'm over-reacting and say, *It's just a bird* ...
>
> If I don't share with you my history, if I don't explain what I've brought with me to this moment in time—that to me the bird hitting the window sounded like a shell detonating—then how could you know me? If I'm shaking, trying to bring myself back to objective reality, saying to myself, *It's a bird, right?* ... and I don't share with you my trauma, I alienate myself. I push you away.
>
> (Wamariya 2018: 219)

Written testimonies of translingual or cross-cultural experiences are significant sources of qualitative data. The effects of these first-person narratives from adults looking back at their reconstructed experiences on both writers and readers have also been studied. As argued in this chapter, writers' published descriptions are not studied as facts. Instead, they are valued for the manner in which they depict writers' conceptualizations of lived crises and of their transformative experiences between languages and cultures. In agreement with Pavlenko (2007), auto-narratives offer readers a glimpse into writers' private worlds, into constructions that are inaccessible via traditional forms of data collection (164–65). Through writers' thematic focus and overall discourse,

BEARING WITNESS TO TRANSLINGUAL REALITIES

we learn about their salient concerns and their attempts to represent affective experiences that rest outside language.

Such narratives symbolize writers' pre-migration traumas and depict what it means to be torn from the comfort of their homes and thrown into confounding realities, become abruptly separated from one's parents, witness the death of loved ones, be exposed to unjustified violence, feel persecuted, and be on the run and homeless. From language socialization and psychoanalytic vantage points, their narratives exhibit the socio-psychological challenges newcomers experience while undergoing their subjective changes: when they experience the guilt of needing to distance themselves from their first loves, and the confusion born from seeing their parents' authority and their values challenged by a dominant society that does not understand their past and their ongoing strife and need for understanding. Equally importantly, their writing also offers illustrations of transformations and inspiring growth.

When examining international relocations, we note that language, aside from having the capacity to destabilize one's reality, also has the ability to heal and even bridge the existential gap of dislocated experiences. As argued by David Denborough (2014), narrating aspects of one's life, or of the lives and experiences of loved ones, relinquishes sufferers' sensed passivity while creating a space for the externalization of socio-affective and psychological difficulties affecting subjects (74–77). Denborough's words echo those of Freud, who, in 'Beyond the pleasure principle', explains that being unwillingly passive when exposed to sudden and/or ongoing danger intensifies subjects' unpleasure (138, 141–42). Writing about our own lives and finding a sense of continuity or linearity in chaos gives meaning to our past and present responses. It also creates a space for us to feel that our concerns are acknowledged and legitimized.

Through testimony and writers' ability to turn passivity into activity, they offset the unpleasant consequences of past confusions and hopelessness. Such acts also create a positive space for healing. These auto-narratives affect writers and readers through their candid descriptions and emphasis on the subjective meaning of trauma and migration. They inform readers about what it is like to feel torn by the tensions exerted between dissimilar languages and cultures, to feel lost and isolated in a new land, and to become burdened by a disorienting reality that dislocates the linearity of their lives, uproots their affect, and confounds and estranges them from their previous selves.

CHILD AND ADOLESCENT MIGRATION, MENTAL HEALTH, AND LANGUAGE

Auto-narratives significantly affect readers, allowing them to witness writers' private lives, their need to share and make sense of their lives, to make them 'logical' and 'real' rather than 'fragmented' and 'distorted' (Wamariya 2018: 33). By sharing their narratives, writers' harrowing stories become validated. Writing helps them make sense of and understand their lives, and move forward through forgiveness.

6 How to Conclude from Here?

> The closest I have ever come to understanding my life in America and my past life in South Africa has been in writing about it.
>
> (Freed 2000: 57)

With a focus on the developmental periods of childhood and adolescence, this volume has drawn the link between migration, trauma, language, and mental health. It examined the effects of early international relocations through psychoanalytic, semiotic, language socialization, and pedagogical lenses. Young migrants', asylum seekers', and refugees' experiences were studied through the interpretation of scholarly and non-scholarly publications, as well as first-person, cross-cultural auto-narratives. Such contributions supported this book's careful study of language's subjective significance and its connection to the psycho-social, developmental, political, and pedagogical challenges impacting minors prior to, during, and following international relocations.

Through the examination of push factors, this volume looked at how pre-migration experiences, relocation journeys, and receiving systems often add to the aetiology of migrants' socio-affective and psychological distress. It highlighted the conditions that often lead to displacements and stressed how migrants' challenges do not always end following their relocations. Attention was also brought to conditions experienced in hotspots, make-shift encampments, government-run refugee camps, and detention centres. We examined parent–child separations, and newcomers' stress over their unknown futures and fear of deportation, and paid close attention to the laws governing receiving systems. We studied how tensions between nations' economic pressures, along with countries' nationalist sentiments, impact destination countries' immigration policies and quota restrictions. And crucially, this book argued that even though there are international laws in place to protect minors' universal rights, practices taking place in several transition and host countries do not always align with minors' pressing needs.

CHILD AND ADOLESCENT MIGRATION, MENTAL HEALTH, AND LANGUAGE

This volume also marked the difference between impersonal, interpersonal, and preconscious traumas. It argued that while impersonal and interpersonal traumas may take root prior to international journeys, while in transit, and/or in the destination countries, preconscious traumas are linked to the condition of migrancy. Founded on psychoanalytic theory, previous chapters also discussed the unconscious, universal trauma infants experience when entering the Symbolic Order. With a consistent focus on migration and mental health, this book stressed that even when individuals are not subjected to unfathomable circumstances taking place prior to and/or during their relocation experiences, following their migration(s), newcomers become negatively impacted by drastic life changes, cumulative crises, and breaks in the universal need for temporal continuity.

In addition, this book emphasized how unaccompanied minors' circumstances differ greatly from the experiences of those who relocate as a family. It stressed how their experiences often involve precarious and/or unsustainable living arrangements, abuse, and/or exploitation. It highlighted how, as seen in the United States under the Trump administration, minors arriving alone also risk deportation. This may occur even if being sent back to their country of origin implies a re-immersion into dangerous and often life-threatening living conditions. When apprehended and not deported, unaccompanied minors are either placed with relatives they may barely know, or in foster care with individuals who may not share their language or culture, and/or may not understand the complexity of their experiences.

In the course of this study we have noted that even when migrations are legal and planned, and when minors relocate safely and accompanied by primary caregivers, international migrations are never perceived by migrants as ordinary occurrences. Becoming immersed within the compounds of a host country and culture involves much more than a mere geographical move and quest for a better life. It is an experience of sudden dislocation that deconstructs everything known to the self. Migrating entails an overwhelming sense of loss and a sudden break in individuals' subjective continuity. It involves the clash between conflicting cultures, belief systems, and languages.

This book thus examined the subjective significance of language, along with the confusion and shock that follows newcomers' initial period of elation (Douglas Brown, cited in Block 2007: 60). It highlighted how our language fulfils a developmental and emotional function in our lives. It is part of an

HOW TO CONCLUDE FROM HERE?

admixture of known and unknown forces that help us make sense of our worlds, influence our behaviours, and develop our sense of self. A symbolic code is an ever-changing phenomenon that marks the connection between our inner and social selves. It links us to our first loves, and to our earliest and later developments as subjects. Our language marks our sense of belonging and/or unbelonging with specific communities of speakers. It is a human trait that becomes entangled with our history of affect. The relation between primary languages and their speakers' master affect becomes evident through the subjective responses each language elicits, and the way it 'prompts emotions, memories, fantasies, projections and identifications' (Kramsch 2009: 2).

Through psychoanalytic and semiotic lenses, this volume focused on an internalized linguistic code's developmental significance. It studied subjects' introjections and projections and how, through seemingly conscious dialogical interactions, individuals respond to the discourse of the Other. The link between language and speakers' meaning-making systems, identity formations, transformations, and re-formations was also explored. We have claimed that speakers' shifting sense of self is influenced and shaped by the beliefs that surround them. Along such lines, this book examined how negative views of migrants knowingly and unknowingly affect their subjectivity. It brought attention to how host societies label migrant groups as foreign threats or problems, and how such labels marginalize and impact the treatment newcomers receive. For minors, such labels affect their self-esteem, social development, mental health, and sense of home. As highlighted by Bemak and Chung (2021):

> [discrimination against newcomers] may relate to differences in food, dress, communication styles, language skills, [accent,] work values and ethics, and personal customs and habits, all of which may be viewed as peculiar and different by the members of the host country. The prejudicial attitudes towards refugees in schools, communities, and in the workplace, may result in assault, harassment, physical and emotional abuse, and robbery, further causing psychological stress and estrangement. (309)

In transit and receiving countries, the stigma attached to migrants is systemic. It places migrants at a disadvantage, affecting different aspects of their lives. Racism and discrimination impact newcomers' ability to access resources and programmes that are meant to aid in their acculturation.[1] At schools, racism and discrimination towards migrants impacts students' self-esteem, academic

119

performance, and life outcomes. Moreover, prejudicial attitudes become infiltrated in, for example, healthcare and justice systems, government policies, and the employment sector. For adults, discrimination against migrants coming from specific regions is observed in the lack of recognition of their educational credentials and their inability to become financially stable through their work.

Popularist modern-day politics across the world have created a culture of fear, rejection, and hatred towards migrants. Anti-refugee and anti-migrant discourse often becomes introjected, whether consciously or unconsciously, by professionals who work with migrant youth and families in the clinical and educational fields (Bemak & Chung 2021: 310–11). Too often, there is an assumption that newcomers bring in diseases, take away jobs, drain resources, and cost taxpayers money that could be applied elsewhere. Migrants are often blamed for increased crime rates. Depending on their background, they are said to be affiliated with gangs or blamed for increased threats of terrorism. These conceptualizations, which are primarily rooted in xenophobia and racism, infringe upon their adjustment and acculturation. In agreement with Bemak and Chung, this 'bombardment of myths and stereotypes' creates an environment of distrust and misunderstandings between newcomers and members of host communities. It not only impacts newcomers' adjustment and acculturation; the proliferation of stereotypes also becomes an added challenge that adds to their stress levels, and infringes upon their well-being and mental health (311). Unfortunately, what many fail to understand is that it is precisely this fear of terrorism, gang affiliations, and criminal acts that becomes a driving force behind individuals' need to emigrate from their home countries.

The harm that stems from the internalization of populist views can be particularly problematic for child and adolescent migrants' sense of self, affiliations, and individuations. While adult migrants may experience a third individuation (Akhtar 1995), children and adolescents first and/or second individuation may become more accentuated. For children and youth, the devaluation of their background may heighten their desire to separate from their parents' values and beliefs. Minors' individuations, combined with their host-language acquisition, may trigger higher stress levels within their homes. The combination of such influences in turn adds to the parent–child conflicts, and to children's conscious and unconscious guilt.

The manner in which the internalization of negative stereotypes impacts newcomers' subjectivity is described by Elamin Abdelmahmoud (2022) in his

HOW TO CONCLUDE FROM HERE?

auto-narrative titled *Son of Elsewhere: A Memoir in Pieces*. When analysing his retrospective experiences as a racialized, first-generation migrant in Ontario, Canada, Abdelmahmoud notes: 'Internalized white supremacy is not the n-word and the pointy hats; it's the wobble in your step, the doubt at the back of your mind' (39). Once again, the problem of stigma, racism, and xenophobia not only lies in the ways in which newcomers may be treated, but also in how such beliefs may knowingly and unknowingly define the way in which migrant children and youth interpret their realities, see themselves, and act.

Central to this project was the analysis of published testimonials as sources of qualitative data. This book has shed light onto the manner in which cross-cultural memoirs disclose the affective side of international relocations, foreign immersions, and fluid identity shifts. The significance of first-person narratives, reconstructed through the lens of time, rests in their propagation of writers' subjective truths.[2] This publication has also revealed how the reconstruction and triangulation of experiences allow for writers to find new meanings, and to understand the feelings that emanate from their past and present circumstances. It has stressed how the act of writing grants writers a sense of agency and healing. Sharing their interpretations of significant events knowingly and unknowingly affords writers a sense of continuity in displacement. Reading first-person accounts of experiences undergone by migrants, moreover, discloses newcomers' resilience while also creating a needed space for understanding and empathy from readers.

This book has also looked at the pedagogical benefits of integrating transcultural auto-narratives in language-learning classrooms. It argues that reading testimonials linked to writers' experiences has the potential to motivate students to read, interpret, and draw parallels with their own occurrences. By increasing relatable in-class discussions, learners may not only reflect on their own memories of linguistic dislocations and cultural (mis)understandings, indeed they may also better understand their past and present and find new meanings therein. Equally importantly, through in-class participation and written engagement, language learners are also given the opportunity to improve their own language skills.

This book's objective

But there remains also the truth that every end in history necessarily contains a new beginning; this beginning is the promise, the only 'message' which the

CHILD AND ADOLESCENT MIGRATION, MENTAL HEALTH, AND LANGUAGE

end can ever produce. Beginning, before it becomes a historical event, is the supreme capacity of man; politically, it is identical with man's freedom.

(Arendt 1985: 478–79)

This volume has sought to provide an interdisciplinary study of the barriers affecting the psycho-social adaptation and acculturation of child and adolescent migrants. With a close look at newcomers' cumulative crises, it examined the importance of taking an epistemological approach to the emerging psycho-emotional and social challenges young migrants often encounter before, during, and following their migrations. Along such lines, it stressed the need for professionals working in the fields of social work, health, counselling, education, government, and policymaking to develop an in-depth understanding of the complexity of newcomers' conditions.

In this time of incessant media coverage of humanitarian crises, members of the public often become immune to stories of massacres, torture, kidnapping, and rape. Many simply grow accustomed to images of war-torn regions and overcrowded vessels detained at countries' points of entry. Many grow accustomed to learning about substandard conditions at refugee camps and makeshift encampments. We have all seen images of capsized boats, as well as children and young families behind barbed wire. In North America, we have been exposed to news of migrants of all ages placed in frigid, cage-like enclosures. Photos and videos of these cramped holding cells have been widely shared, not as a humanitarian call for change, but for the purpose of discouraging people from crossing the Mexico–USA border illegally. Added to such images are stories of children who are torn from their caregivers and thrown into systems that, once again, do not lend themselves to these minors' psycho-social well-being, positive adjustment, and healthy development.

Some international relocations are celebrated as triumphs by organizations and countries that try to help refugees and asylum seekers. Yet the experiences of many displaced children and adolescents who have not been granted legal entries often go unnoticed or ignored. In agreement with Measham et. al (2014), 'Providing care and support to refugee children and their families ... [should be a] world-wide concern' (208). Nevertheless, international efforts have proven insufficient in addressing our growing humanitarian crises. While destination countries such as Canada attempt to increase refugee quotas, most international efforts have barely limited the impact of this escalating, global problem.

HOW TO CONCLUDE FROM HERE?

The challenges experienced by migrants are not restricted to faraway lands and remote shores. As argued throughout this book, human suffering does not always end when minors and families relocate. In transit and destination countries, newcomers are affected by their personal and shared histories of displacement and relocation. They are also impacted by the cumulative stressors that are commonly linked to systemic discrimination and racism.

As stated by Bemak and Chung (2021), a political climate that fosters hatred, fear, racism, discrimination, and xenophobia adds to newcomers' stress and process of acculturation (310). In both transit and host countries, we must question the dominant discourse labelling newcomers and discrediting their struggles and needs. It is important to consider that while media outlets bring attention to this global crisis, often such outlets also propagate messages that lend to fear and even hatred towards—racialized—migrants. Likewise, professionals working with newcomers should account for the ways in which dominant stereotypes may influence their work, and how comments and/or silences may contribute to the prevalence of this growing problem.

Post-traumatic growth is increased when individuals benefit from a reliable support system. By contrast, experiencing discrimination and marginalization inflicts upon newcomers' adjustment and healthy psychological functioning. The stress newcomers experience while trying to adjust in a new country 'is more predictive of psychological problems than traumas experienced before relocating' (Measham et al. 2014: 208–09). Minors' post-migration struggles affect their ability to establish healthy socio-emotional attachments with members of the dominant culture and with individuals who share their language and/or heritage culture. Added to the challenges child and adolescent migrants may experience at schools are the anxieties and overall concerns that may exist at home. Since parental stress and mental health contribute to minors' well-being (208), adults' overall experiences and the dynamics taking place in minors' homes should never be disregarded.

Where Do We Go from Here?

There is no simple solution to eradicating world famine, hatred, discrimination, persecution, corruption, or violence. Likewise, in spite of wealthy countries' efforts to combat climate change, displacements caused by environmental disasters continue to rise. Open-door policies have been perceived as unsustainable in receiving countries. While there is no clear and simple answer to the problems listed thus far, there is something that can be done in transit and destination countries. Our involvement in the global response to our ongoing humanitarian crisis can start at home.

The mental health and well-being of newcomers must be taken into consideration from their first point of contact with the relocation country. Informed, culturally responsive approaches at schools and within healthcare and justice systems are imperative in supporting young migrants' positive mental health outcomes and post-traumatic growth. Professionals in the areas of mental health, medicine, social work, and education should be made aware of the challenges undergone by young newcomers and families prior to, during, and following their international relocations.

As argued in this volume, relocation experiences

> result in unresolved psychological challenges during resettlement ... [and place refugees at a] higher risk for developing serious health problems ... greater degrees of generalized anxiety, ... psychosis, dissociation, and higher rates of psychopathology when compared to the general population. (Bemak & Chung 2021: 307)

Amalgamated with relocation challenges is the ongoing concern over the well-being of people they were forced to leave behind, and/or the grief of those they may have lost.

It is essential for healthcare professionals to understand the nuances of how trauma, migration, and discrimination interact to create a unique set of difficulties for minors. As argued by Measham et al. (2014), 'children may also express distress in ways that do not fit with prevailing diagnostic paradigms, and the identification and management of their difficulties may be complicated by selective mutism, speech or learning disorders, or other constitutional issues' (209). Working with members of migrant communities to develop trauma-informed care and culturally informed interventions is crucial.

As highlighted thus far,

> Refugee children are at risk for mental health difficulties including post-traumatic stress disorder (PTSD) and depression, as well as other ... emotional and behavioural issues, disturbed sleep, nightmares, grief reactions, inattention, social withdrawal, and medically unexplained symptoms. (209)

HOW TO CONCLUDE FROM HERE?

Consequently, increased support should also stem from communities and schools, ensuring that the needs of unaccompanied minors and the needs of young families are met.

For unaccompanied minors, culturally responsive foster care and community placements, as well as mentorship programmes, are crucial to their adjustment, acculturation, and healthy developmental growth. This book also discussed how some unaccompanied minors are willing agents, and as such, they are not misled into the sex-trade industry. Yet whether minors are willing participants or victims, they are nonetheless susceptible to the traumas caused prior to and through their post-migration experiences. Thus, in both transit and destination countries, initiatives that aim at identifying, combating, and reducing the impact of trafficking are necessary.

Educating and assessing the scope of this human trafficking and exploitation is unquestionably vital. Hence, anti-human-trafficking training for immigration agents and, within countries' borders, training for front-line police officers should be mandatory. Increased funding should be allocated to train social workers, mental health professionals, doctors, and nurses assisting this vulnerable sector of migrant populations. Countries should increase victim-centred programmes and linkage to community support. Individuals in transit and destination countries need to be educated on this growing concern. Citizens should be able to anonymously report suspicions of trafficking. Moreover, stricter national and international laws should be in place, so that those directly and indirectly implicated in this crime are made accountable.[3]

We understand that minors' positive adaptation, resilience, and psycho-emotional well-being depend on the establishment and maintenance of a supportive home. In other words, children and youth need nurturing environments that uphold positive communication. For accompanied minors, there are benefits to upholding family cohesion, maintaining their heritage language, and establishing a balance between heritage values and customs and those of the relocation country (Burgos, Al-Adeimi & Brown 2019: 429–31). As argued by Burgos, Al-Adeimi, and Brown, 'greater parental warmth ... [is linked] to less experiences of depression and fewer psychological symptoms ... Contrarily, symptoms of depression ... increase among youth with higher levels of parental overprotection' (431). The problem, however, is that given migrants' strenuous circumstances, this ideal, cohesive, understanding, and nurturing environment

CHILD AND ADOLESCENT MIGRATION, MENTAL HEALTH, AND LANGUAGE

may be difficult to uphold. An added concern is parental overprotection and rejection of host values.

Primary caregivers, who may also experience negative encounters with members of the host culture, may be less inclined to accept dominant cultures' views and behaviours. Furthermore, since adults may be more likely employed in sectors where ethnic languages are spoken, their acquisition of the host language may be limited. This, by extension, limits adults' positive interactions with members of the receiving culture and increases their need and willingness to interact with individuals who share their same background and/or language. For adults, the greater the discrimination and isolation from the dominant culture, the greater is the idealization of their heritage language and culture. When this occurs, migrants tend to uphold and enforce their values, while rejecting those of the host culture. This, in turn, increases the stress levels in the home.

Likewise, when addressing the challenges affecting migrant parents and their children, Bemak and Chung (2021) note:

> It is common for refugee children to acclimate more quickly, acquiring language and understanding new social norms more rapidly than their caretakers and subsequently causing significant changes in family relationships, especially if children begin to challenge their caretakers about their traditional beliefs, values, and behaviours ... Consequently, for some refugee caretakers and parents, confusion arises about acceptable normative behaviours such as childrearing and discipline practices. Longstanding and established roles within the family become unclear, especially if the new rules and behaviours are inconsistent with their cultural values and beliefs. Given faster acquisition of language, children often become the language and cultural interpreters and therefore disrupt the traditional family hierarchy ... Adding to the changing family dynamics are children wanting to more 'fully' acculturate, questioning traditional roles and norms, as they adopt the ways of the new culture ... [This in turn causes] a redefinition and role confusion in families, changed relationships, family dysfunction, and painful family restructuring. (308–09)

Another reason for decreased parent–child communication and family cohesion may be linked to children's empathy. As Burgos, Al-Adeimi, and Brown describe, 'Youth are found to be aware and understand the daily pressures experienced by their parents ... [hence,] they can be reluctant in asking their parents for help and can speak restrictively about their concerns' (2019: 431).

HOW TO CONCLUDE FROM HERE?

As minors' awareness of their parents' struggles become prominent, their children, in an effort to not add to their parents' stress, may avoid sharing their concerns. As parent–child communication decreases, minors may turn to members of their extended families and/or friends for support. While minors may benefit from the support of such adults and peers, problems do arise when those influencing and offering support do not have minors' best interests in mind.

For young migrants, balancing a support system that involves friends from their heritage background and from the dominant group is important. So is the attempt to uphold open communication within the family system. Parents' exposure to the host culture and language is necessary for their own acculturation. As argued thus far, it is also significant for caregivers to understand the changes and challenges their children experience. Learning the host language, however possible, may allow for caregivers to learn about the new culture and remain actively involved in their children's lives. Acquiring the host language increases parents' social and navigational capital. It may allow parents to establish a fruitful balance between their social ties with members of their own heritage community and those of the host culture. Needless to say, acquiring the host language may also result in greater employment opportunities, self-sufficiency, and, by extension, less financial stress.

Acculturation could pose a challenge when, in the relocation country, newcomers are exposed to racism and xenophobia. Discrimination, added to unresolved pre- and post-migration traumas, depression and, potentially, survivors' guilt, exacerbates the complexity of acculturation and adjustment for newcomers in resettlement countries (Bemak & Chung 2021: 308). For newcomers trying to build a new life, finding support systems that help them work through such challenges is crucial. Feeling a sense of safety and security in the resettlement country and having opportunities that are equitable and lend to their financial self-sufficiency are significant for adults' acculturation and the well-being of the family as a whole.

Greater attention should be given to the need to challenge racialization and racism and their link to newcomers' low wages and underemployment. Funds should be allocated to help with newcomers' mental health concerns, to support employment training programmes, and to aid in their financial struggles, housing concerns, and legal fees. Given that schools and schoolyards are environments affected by the dichotomies of social growth and setbacks,

CHILD AND ADOLESCENT MIGRATION, MENTAL HEALTH, AND LANGUAGE

acceptance and marginalization, learning and unlearning, attention to school-based support, as well as counsellor and teacher training on equity, cultural competence, and anti-racism strategies should be at the forefront of countries' approach to integrating migrant students.

In schools, having practices of support in place and increasing the awareness of circumstances that may affect children's home environments would be of great significance to students' development and positive adjustment. Prioritizing the development of Individual Education Plans (IEP), ensuring age-appropriate placements with extra learning support, and providing students with counselling are also conducive to students' resilience and positive growth. For older students affected by the added stress of financial responsibilities, alternative school arrangements should also be made available to support their education.

At the elementary and secondary school levels, incorporating diversity into the curricula with reading material that is relatable to newcomers is also essential. Integrating topics that are of relevance to students, such as social justice, equity, human rights, and intercultural communication would empower students, motivate their learning, and tap into their potential as global citizens. It is important for educators to develop cultural competence and sensitivity to ongoing power dynamics experienced within and outside the classrooms. Equally importantly, educators should be aware of the emotionality of language learning. They should also be sensitive to the difficulties students often encounter through differences in culture, belief systems, behaviours, expectations, teaching styles, and learning approaches. Establishing social support systems through in-school and after-school programmes is also vital.

Conclusion

As argued throughout this book's final chapter, protecting children's and adolescents' mental health and well-being requires knowledge, attentiveness, sensitivity, and responsibility from everyone. It is not just the responsibility of educators, school administrators, and guidance counsellors. It involves awareness and knowledge from doctors, nurses, psychologists, psychiatrists, and social workers. It entails community-mindedness, understanding, and sensibility from members of migrant and non-migrant communities alike. Defying stereotypes and amplifying our awareness of the difficulties minors and entire

HOW TO CONCLUDE FROM HERE?

families often encounter before and following their migration would also make a promising start. Increasing funding in the areas of mental health and wellness and making therapy available to both children and their parents should be understood not as a commodity, but a right. Once again, it is essential to support extracurricular, culturally sensitive programmes in community centres, especially in neighbourhoods with high concentrations of ethnic groups.

Aiding in minors' acculturation and providing them with fair opportunities for their socio-emotional growth is vital to countries' short- and long-term sociocultural and economic competence. Host communities need to become open-minded to the benefits of inclusion and diversity. Hiring individuals of diverse backgrounds, who are representative of minority groups within the educational, health, social, and even justice systems, is also key to countries' inclusion, prosperity, and change. In transit and destination countries, educating everyone, especially those in a position to help, should not be out of reach.

Post-secondary programmes in the fields of health sciences, education, national and international politics, and legislation should be encouraged to include courses that cover the extenuating challenges that many migrant populations encounter. Such an approach would make a valuable difference to newcomers' experiences. Hopefully, it could translate into ensuring that, in time, receiving countries become more adept at welcoming and helping newcomers' social integration and growth. Awareness of the challenges children and migrant families encounter has the potential to increase receiving societies' tolerance and acceptance. Looking critically at the stigma of migration and questioning stereotypes would allow for transit and host societies to value newcomers' sociocultural, economic, political, and professional integration. It could also lead to a better understanding of migrants' potential, and an appreciation of them as the newest members of our growing and ever-changing societies.

Notes

Introduction

1 A term I have come across due to recent global events is 'climate refugees'. This term refers to individuals displaced by environmental disasters, droughts, and events that stem from our global change in climate. Individuals displaced by climate change and resulting natural disasters are not endorsed by the United Nations High Commissioner for Refugees (UNHCR).

2 To grow up in migrancy refers to the experience lived both by children who have moved from their country of birth, and children who were born into transnational families.

CHAPTER 1—Dialogic Encounters: Conceptualizing Effects on Belief Systems, Subjectivities, and Individuals' Personal and Shared Histories

1 The latter part of the sentence is taken from 'What Remains? The Language Remains', where Arendt refers to the teachings of Karl Jaspers, her former professor (Baehr 2000: 21).

2 Note to readers: the given quotes are not offered in chronological order. Instead, Arendt's citations are listed according to this section's themes within the discourse on language.

3 Within this discourse, the word canonization is used to describe subjects' mere repetitions of alien (others') utterances. Such speech acts resist change or modification which, by lacking the freedom of subjects' re-accentuation, deters speakers' coming to consciousness (385–86, 417).

4 According to Bakhtin, coming-to-consciousness refers to subjects' assimilation into their own system of meanings and the simultaneous liberation of their own words from the authoritative discourse that surrounds them (344).

5 Uvira is a city in the South Kivu Province of the Democratic Republic of Congo.

NOTES

6 For example, individuals affected by endemic poverty and generalized violence.

7 While hard violence is physical, soft violence is psychological or symbolic. Hard violence is easier to identify. Soft violence is 'often more elusive but may be equally devastating in the long run' (Suárez-Orozco & Robben 2000: 1; as cited in Ensor 2016: 72).

8 An asylum seeker is a person claiming to be a refugee whose status, however, is yet to be verified and processed.

9 Turkey and Greece are examples of transit states. Due to their geographic location, these countries become a gateway to other destinations. As argued by Hodes et al. (2018), their physical location makes these asylum countries a major entry point to more affluent countries within the European Union (391). Not all transit states have a coastline. Countries that neighbour the areas of conflict may also be defined as transit states. This chapter makes a clear distinction between a transit state—or country—and a host or resettlement country. Mexico is a transit and host country to migrants coming from more impoverished countries. Mexico is also a country of national emigrants. The United States, for the most part, is a host country. With minimal exceptions in undocumented migrants travelling from the United States to Canada, adults, families, and unaccompanied minors who legally and illegally relocate to the United States from or through Mexico intend to make the USA their final destination.

10 Germany's response to the 2015 Syrian crisis made it a model receiving country within the European Union. Its open-door policy, however, ended in 2018 when the country's conservative parties pressed the German government to secure its borders. Following the change, Germany continued to provide health and psycho-social services for migrants who were already within its borders, while restricting the entrance to future arrivals.

11 By separating from their parents, children were labelled 'unaccompanied' and were either placed with family members living in the USA or placed in shelters or foster care.

12 The Flores Settlement Agreement is a nationwide policy for the detention, release, and treatment of accompanied and unaccompanied minors in the United States. Unless children are expeditiously removed, this policy requires minors in federal custody to be placed in non-secure, state-licensed facilities within days or—during influx—weeks of their apprehension (Herman-Peck & Harrington 2018: 119, 121).

13 Children who cross borders illegally cross as accompanied or unaccompanied minors. Accompanied minors travel with at least one parent or legal guardian. Unaccompanied minors, on the other hand, travel alone. As maintained by Goździak (2016), even though most unaccompanied children are agents exercising

NOTES

their free will to cross state borders illegally, their journeys are commonly financed by parents and/or loved ones (26–27) who hope their children's relocation will enable a break from the determinism that grounds their relentless condition.

CHAPTER 2—Migration and Trauma: Defining the Problem of Child and Adolescent Transnational Relocations

1 With the European Commission's assistance, Greece has activated hotspots in Chios, Kos, Lesvos, Leros, and Samos. In Italy, hotspots have been established in Pozzallo, Taranto, and Trapani (Tazzioli 2017: 2765).

2 When approved, their destination within Europe is not a choice for newcomers. Migrants are sent through specific pathways to specified locations. Depending on established agreements, those approved are allowed passage to EU countries that have agreed to absorb pre-determined rates of asylum seekers (Tazzioli 2017: 2765).

3 As explained in this section and stressed by Tazzioli (2017), to qualify for international protection, migrants need to prove a fear of persecution. If they come from a war-torn country or are, for example, religious minorities fearing persecution, their application for asylum is considered. If, however, individuals come from impoverished countries, or if they have been displaced by environmental disasters, including persistent droughts and inability to access water or food, then migrants' applications for international protection are denied (2769, 2771).

4 According to Tazzioli 2017, on average, the process takes between two and three weeks (2770). Unlike Italian authorities that 'have no intentions of keeping migrants' (2772), in the Greek Islands, migrants may wait for a year or longer until their asylum claim is processed (2770, 2773). This time frame expands for those who challenge their deportation to Turkey. In such cases, waiting times in Greece substantially exceed the one-year frame.

5 As part of the 2016 EU–Turkey Joint Action Plan, Turkey has agreed to help with the flow of irregular migration to Europe by taking back inadmissible migrants that came through the Turkey–Europe route. As part of the agreement, for every Syrian returned to Turkey from the Greek Islands, the EU is to resettle a qualified Syrian asylum seeker into Europe. This arrangement also includes the European Union's distribution of €3 billion for concrete projects to help refugees in Turkey. Special attention is to be paid to women, children, and other vulnerable groups such as religious minorities—e.g. Christians and Yazidis. In addition, part of the funds is meant to address gender-related violence and abuse against women and children on the migrant crossing routes from Turkey. Another salient component of this joint plan is for both parties to work to improve humanitarian conditions

NOTES

inside Syria (http://www.europarl.europa.eu/legislative-train/theme-towards-a-new-policy-on-migration/file-eu-turkey-statement-action-plan). As argued by Elizabeth Collett (2016), the problem with such an arrangement is that not all asylum seekers travelling through Turkey to Greece are from Syria. Many are from other countries, such as Afghanistan and Iraq. The 2016 bilateral action plan does not offer sustainable protection for non-Syrian entrants (40).

6 Overcrowding, poor living conditions, frustration, and violence involving minors at camps have been well covered by the media. The article 'Minor killed at Moira migrant camp on Lesbos' (Sanderson 2019) offers a concrete example. This online publication describes the violent outburst that took place in August 2019 at a camp in Lesbos, Greece. During a violent clash, a fifteen-year-old boy from Afghanistan lost his life, while two other boys were seriously injured. Aside from overcrowding and prolonged stays, this article highlights the call by the UN refugee agency (UNHCR) for the Greek government to transfer unaccompanied and accompanied minors to safer places (Sanderson 2019: paras 1, 3–4).

7 In their 2017 publication, Linton, Griffin, and Shapiro claim that such shelters offer 'dormitory-style rooms, shared bathrooms, showers, clothes, and hot meals. These places also offer year-around educational services, recreational facilities, and limited legal services'. In 2015, the average length of stay in shelters was thirty-four days, although some children remained in custody for longer periods. Upon entry into these facilities, children receive an initial medical and mental health evaluation. While in custody, moreover, children receive mental and health services either on- or off-site (4).

8 An adult's release depends on factors such as being deemed a flight risk, a danger to the public, and establishing their identity sufficiently (Herman-Peck & Harrington 2018: 114). Often, a release may take place under specific court-established conditions, such as having the adult wear an electronic monitor (Linton, Griffin & Shapiro 2017: 5), or releasing the adult on bond.

9 In April 2018, the 'zero-tolerance policy' of persecuting illegal migrants in the United States was announced. When entering the United States surreptitiously, aside from immigration proceedings, subjects may be subjected to criminal proceedings for violating the country's immigration laws (Herman-Peck & Harrington 2018: 124).

10 When detained, all individuals are subjected to expeditious removal—deportation without immigration hearings—unless they request asylum and pass fear of persecution interviews. If apprehended individuals are able to demonstrate such fears and thus pass the interview, migrants are subjected to standard removal proceedings with immigration hearings (Herman-Peck & Harrington 2018: 110).

NOTES

11 Shelters and residential centres in the United States are operated by the Department of Health and Human Services (DHH) under the care of the Office of Refugee Resettlement (ORR) (Linton, Griffin & Shapiro 2017: 2).

12 As published by the Global Detention Project, in Canada, the demand for space at holding centres is so high that authorities often feel pressured to temporarily incarcerate adult migrants in medium-security prisons (2018: 7). The Toronto Star has highlighted that aside from the space problem, provincial prisons are also used to hold higher-risk detainees (Bensadoun 2019: para. 7).

13 The Global Detention Project (GDP) is a non-profit research centre based in Geneva, Switzerland, that investigates the use of immigration-related detention as a response to global migration.

14 Vulnerable individuals include children, pregnant women, nursing mothers, elderly individuals, persons with physical disabilities and/or mental health concerns, and individuals suffering from chronic, debilitating illnesses (Global Detention Project 2018: 11).

15 Canada has no maximum immigration detention times. According to 2016 reports, the average length of detention in Canada was 19.5 days, which is the median duration compared to other key destination countries—six months in Australia, thirty-five days in the United States, and ten days in France. Regardless of the average, the longest immigration detention in Canada was nine years. The second longest, to date, was seven years (Global Detention Project 2018: 12).

16 Between 2012 and 2017, 36–40% of all immigration detainees, including individuals with mental healthcare concerns, were placed in maximum-security provincial jails (Global Detention Project 2018: 2, 12, 19).

17 While the United States refers to illegal migrants as 'aliens', Canada uses the term 'foreign nationals' to define non-naturalized citizens who have entered the country illegally or have extended and therefore violated the length and/or terms of their stay in Canada. That being said, the classification of unaccompanied and accompanied minors, asylum seekers, refugees, and economic and environmental migrants remains, in its general sense, consistent across countries.

18 The grounds for detention and release are provided in subsections 55–60 of the Immigration and Refugee Protection Act (IRPA) (5).

19 Factors that determine whether an individual is a flight risk and is thus less likely to present themselves for examinations, at proceedings, or for removal may include suspicion of being a fugitive, suspicion of being involved in human smuggling or trafficking, having arrived through an irregular entry as part of a group smuggled into the country with links to terrorism, having destroyed identity or travel documents, lacking an established identity, having provided contradictory information,

NOTES

not cooperating with authorities, and having strong ties with a community in Canada (pp. 5–6).

20 Canada has three detention holding centres: one in Toronto, Ontario; one in Laval, Quebec; and one in Vancouver, British Columbia. These are located near or, as in Vancouver, within its international airports.

CHAPTER 3—Memory within Language: Our Mother Tongue's Link to our Subjective Development and our Remembered and Seemingly Forgotten Sense of Being, Loving, and Belonging

1 In his 1969–70 seminar, Lacan re-examines the Oedipus complex, and analyses the myth of Oedipus as one of Freud's dreams.

2 Instead of the pseudo-Freudian reification of the bourgeois nuclear family, Lacan assigned sociocultural positions to persons involved within the child's Oedipal triangulation. According to Lacan, individuals of any sex/gender take on maternal and paternal roles (Johnston 2022). That being said, as with most discussions involving Lacan's work, this publication still refers to the primary caregiver as the mother and the child's paternal figure as the father.

3 The description of the Oedipal Complex has always been gender specific. Nevertheless, for the section and throughout this publication, gender neutral pronouns are used.

4 This term, which in French means enjoyment, is used by Lacan when describing the early period in which the child begins to discover their mother's sexuality. Linked to prohibition, this 'painful pleasure' is experienced before and throughout the period in which the potential rival—the father—has entered the child's experience (Akhtar 2009: 155, 167).

5 For this theory, 'to wean' does not correspond to breastfeeding. By weaning Winnicott means the mother's task of gradually disillusioning the infant, thus making them understand that there is a reality outside the self and that external reality is not under the child's omnipotent control (13).

6 Focusing on the anatomy of the brain, van der Kolk and van der Hart state that our human brain becomes more ridged—ceases to adapt and change—with myelinization. Following this post-pubescent developmental stage, attachment patterns, as well as speech, become established (1995: 172).

7 According to Stengel, the level of anxiety and the degree of (dis)comfort language learners experience when learning a new language is tied to age. Older individuals feel more inhibited during the initial stages of foreign-language learning (477).

NOTES

8 Hegemonic relations founded on language fluency and native-like accent is intimately linked to Foucault's post-structural view on language and power (Carra-Salsberg 2017: 17).

9 Here we must note that while members of dominant groups may stigmatize migrants, migrants who are also survivors of trauma may widen this unfortunate gap. As discussed in this book's fourth chapter, it is not uncommon for children and even grandchildren of survivors to be affected by the aftermath of the significant event. Along such lines and founded on his interpretation of Kleinian theory, Volkan suggests that through the process of projective identification, survivors pass their trauma to successive generations. These transmissions support the idea of children as 'reservoirs for the extremely traumatized image of their parental figures' (Volkan 2017: 87). As seen with Holocaust survivors, the significant event becomes the 'large group identity marker' that affects the manner in which those who do not belong to their group are perceived (87–88).

CHAPTER 4—Trauma's Dimension within and outside Language

1 This hate may also be targeted at imaginary or famous figures. In our current world, the latter may involve individuals seen on television or through social media, for example. Guided by Anna Freud's (1936) theory, Klein suggests that for adolescents, since protecting those close to their heart lessens their anxiety and guilt, hating imaginary, famous, or remote individuals is the least dangerous path in teenagers' unconscious minds. These distantly real or imagined individuals are inaccessible and remote to the child and are therefore the safest to hate (Klein & Riviere 1964: 97–98).

2 Drawing from Pierre Janet's (1989) work, van der Kolk and van der Hart affirm that 'Memories easily become inaccurate when new ideas and pieces of information are combined with old knowledge to form flexible mental schemas.' As claimed by Janet: 'Once a particular event or bit of information becomes integrated in a larger scheme, it is no longer accessible as an individual entity, and hence, the memory will be distorted' (cited in van der Kolk and van der Hart 1995: 171).

CHAPTER 5—Bearing Witness to Translingual Realities: A Study of the Significance of First-Person, Cross-Cultural Publications

1 With a focus on girls' development and Freud's early teachings, we note that, as with boys, a girl's first love object is her mother. Yet, between the ages of three and

NOTES

five, the female infant becomes aware of that which she lacks—the phallic signifier. This lack, continues Freud, makes the young girl resent her mother, and before identifying with her mother once again, the girl switches her love object to her father (Freud 1931: 226–28). In agreement with Clara Thompson (1943), one may assume that more than 'a biological lack', Freud's understanding of a girl's 'penis envy' is also linked to the symbolic, for it symbolizes the patriarchal order (124).

2 According to Paola Bohórquez-Arcila, 'translingualism' is defined as a psycho-emotional and linguistic condition of living in transition between two or more symbolic codes. A translingual subject is an individual who experiences an imbalance between languages (2008: 2). For this research, translingual literature refers to narratives written by first-, 1.5 and/or second-generation migrants who live or have lived through the abovementioned inner state of transition. 1.5-generation migrants are children of first-generation migrants. Even though they are born in the host country, they only learn the dominant language when entering the host school system.

3 The 18th Annual Day of Applied Linguistics Conference, titled Strange Lands: Location and Dislocation: The Immigrant Experience. University of Toronto, 15 September 2012.

4 Akhtar argues that displacement, a term that originated from Sigmund Freud (1894a), refers to the redirecting of psychic energy from one idea to another. It is a primary mental process that 'underlies the formation of symbols, symptoms, and the manifest content of dreams'. Relational displacement is one of four types of unconscious shift. Relational displacement changes an instinctual drive's object while retaining its aim (e.g. hating or loving one person is shifted into hating or loving another person) (82).

5 This was arranged so Wamariya could be closer to her school. Based on descriptions provided in the memoir, even though Wamariya called Mrs Thomas her 'American mother', the arrangement does not seem to be one of foster care or adoption (54).

6 Britzman (2006) defines the third space as an area in which self–other interactions become governed by an unconsciously shared 'give and take'. It is a terrain through which we unknowingly respond to others' psychic histories and resulting affect as much as others respond to our own history of affect (42–44, 49). Britzman's definition is of significant value to our understanding of language: since our symbolic code of meanings becomes an interactive, propelling, and encoding register, we cannot disregard our tongue's inevitable implication within this space, especially after accounting for the way in which language holds together our known and unknown histories, perceptions, and experiences that mark our responses towards and interpretations of others and of ourselves in relation to others.

NOTES

CHAPTER 6—How to Conclude from Here?

1 For newcomers, the phases of the acculturation process include assimilation, integration/biculturalism, rejection, and deculturation (Berry 2003). Berry argues that integration/biculturalism is the healthiest period of acculturation. It combines adjustment to a new country with 'concurrently integrating traditional beliefs and values' (cited in Bemak & Chung 2021: 308).

2 As examined earlier, memories of early events and of stressful events may reflect realities that vary from what has been encoded by others. Fivush and Nelson (2020) argue that these differences reflect individuals' interpretation of the event(s), along with the feelings experienced through the occurrence. These variations may relate to how similar newer experiences may be to earlier ones—specifically, to how both the earlier and the later events may elicit similar feelings and as such, become stored and integrated together. To quote Pierre Janet (1989): 'Once a particular event or bit of information becomes integrated in a larger scheme, it is no longer accessible as an individual entity, and hence, the memory will be distorted' (cited in van der Kolk & van der Hart 1995: 171). Such variations or distortions nevertheless do not impact on the importance of writers' narratives.

3 An indirect involvement with human trafficking may include persons who witness and fail to report the crime. Hotel employees, as an example, could fall under this category. Even if they may not benefit from this organized criminal act, by not contacting authorities they become facilitators.

References

Abdelmahmoud, E. (2022). *Son of Elsewhere: A Memoir in Pieces*. New York: Random House.

Agamben, G. (1999). *Remnants of Auschwitz: The Witness and the Archive*. New York: Zone Books.

Agosín, M. (2003). Words: A basket of love. In S.G. Kellman (ed.), *Switching Languages: Translingual Writers Reflect on their Craft* (pp. 319–26). Lincoln: University of Nebraska Press.

Akhtar, S. (1995). A third individuation: immigration, identity, and the psychoanalytic process. *Journal of American Psychoanalytic Association*, 43(4), 1051–84.

——— (2009). *Comprehensive Dictionary in Psychoanalysis*. London: Karnac Books.

——— (2012). *Strange Lands: Location and Dislocation: The Immigrant Experience*. Presented at the 18th Annual Day in Applied Psychoanalysis, Toronto, Ontario, 15 September.

Amezcua, S. (2019). Familias separadas: the zero tolerance policy that changed the U.S. immigration system. *Bard Digital Commons*. https://digitalcommons.bard.edu/cgi/viewcontent.cgi?article=1044&context=senproj_s2019

Ang, S., Ho, E., Yeoh, B. (2022). Migration and new racism beyond colour and the "West": co-ethnicity, intersectionality and postcoloniality. *Ethnic and Racial Studies*, 45(4), 585–594. https://doi.org/10.1080/01419870.2021.1925321

Arendt, H. (1985). *The Origins of Totalitarianism*. New York: Harcourt Brace.

——— (1993). *Men in Dark Times*. New York: Harcourt Brace.

——— (1998). *The Human Condition*. Chicago: University of Chicago Press.

Baehr, P.R. (2000). 'What remains? The language remains': a conversation with Günter Gaus. In P.R. Baehr (ed.), *The Portable Hannah Arendt* (pp. 3–22). Toronto: Penguin.

Bakhtin, M.M. (1981). *The Dialogic Imagination: Four Essays by M.M. Bakhtin*, ed. M. Holquist, trans. C.Emerson and M. Holquist. Austin: University of Texas Press.

Baranczak, S. (1996). Tongue tied eloquence: Note on language, exile and writing. In M. Robinson (ed.), *Altogether Elsewhere: Writers on Exile* (pp. 242–251). New York: Harcourt Brace.

REFERENCES

BBC (2022). What are President Biden's challenges at the Mexico border? BBC News, 28 June. https://www.bbc.com/news/world-us-canada-56255613 (accessed 4 November 2021)

Begley, L. (2005). On being an orphaned writer. In W. Lesser (ed.), *The Genius of Language: Fifteen Writers Reflect on their Mother Tongues.* Toronto: Anchor Books.

Bemak, F.D., & Chung, R.C.-Y. (2021). A culturally responsive intervention for modern-day refugees: a multiphase model of psychotherapy, social justice, and human rights. In J.D. Aten & J. Hwang (eds), *Refugee Mental Health* (pp. 103–36). Washington, DC: American Psychological Association.

Bensadoun, E. (2019). How immigration detention centres work in Canada. *The Canadian Press/Toronto Star.* https://www.ctvnews.ca/canada/how-immigration-detention-centres-work-in-canada-1.4497688 (Accessed 23 November 2023).

Bion, W. (1962). *Learning from Experience.* New York: Basic Books.

Blanchot, M (1995). *The Writing of the Disaster,* trans. A. Smock. Lincoln: University of Nebraska Press.

Block, D. (2007). *Second Language Identities.* New York: Continuum.

Bohórquez-Arcila, P. (2008). *Living between Languages: Linguistic Exile and Self Translation.* Doctoral dissertation. http://search.proquest.com.ezproxy.library.yorku.ca/docview/305041433(Accessed 4 January 2019).

Britzman, D. (2006). *Novel Education: Psychoanalytic Studies of Learning and Not Learning.* New York: Peter Lang.

Britzman, D., & Pitt, A. (2004). Pedagogy and clinical knowledge: some psychoanalytic observations on losing and refinding significance. *JAC Online,* 24, 353–74. http://www.jaconlinejournal.com/archives/vol24.2.html (Accessed 27 March 2021).

Burgos, M., Al-Adeimi, M., & Brown, J. (2019). Needs of newcomer youth. *Child and Adolescent Social Work Journal,* 36(4), 429–37. https://doi.org/10.1007/s10560-018-0571-3

Butler, J. (2009). *Frames of War: When Is Life Grievable?* London: Verso.

Camus, A. (1996). The rains of New York. In In M. Robinson (ed.), *Altogether Elsewhere: Writers on Exile* (pp. 307–10). New York: Harcourt Brace.

Cariola, L. (2017). Defense mechanism. In V. Zeigler-Hill & T.K. Shakelford (eds), *Encyclopedia of Personality and Individual Differences.* https://doi.org/10.1007/978-3-319-28099-8

Carra-Salsberg, F. (2015a). Aggression and the telos of learning: a psychoanalytic study of significant language learning. *Journal of Language and Psychoanalysis,* 4(2), 34–49. https://doi.org/10.7565/landp.2015v2

———. (2015b). Impressions and transformations: a psychoanalytic study of the effects of early linguistic disruptions, emotional trauma, and of testimony through

REFERENCES

the study of Oscar Hijuelos' *Thoughts without Cigarettes*. *Journal of Language and Psychoanalysis*, 4(1), 31–49. https://doi.org/10.7565/landp.2015v1

——— (2017). A psychoanalytic look into the effects of childhood and adolescent migration in Eva Hoffman's *Lost in Translation*. *Journal of Language and Psychoanalysis*, 6(1), 10–32. http://www.language-and-psychoanalysis.com/article/view/1837/pdf_31(Accessed 20 January 2022).

Caruth, C. (1995). *Trauma: Explorations in Memory*. Baltimore, MD: John Hopkins University Press.

——— (1996). Freud, Moses and monotheism. In C. Caruth (ed.), *Unclaimed Experience: Trauma, Narrative, and History*. (pp. 10–24). Baltimore, MD: Johns Hopkins University Press.

Cheatham, A., & Roy, D. (n.d.). *What is Canada's immigration policy?* Council on Foreign Relations. https://www.cfr.org/backgrounder/what-canadas-immigration-policy

Collett, E. (2016). EU cooperation with third countries: rethinking concepts and investments. *Forced Migration Review: Destination Europe*, 51, 17–19. https://www.fmreview.org/sites/fmr/files/FMRdownloads/en/destination-europe.pdf (accessed 5 December 2019).

Convention of the Rights of the Child (1989). *United Nations Human Rights Office of the High Commissioner*. https://www.ohchr.org/en/professionalinterest/pages/crc.aspx(Accessed 30 April 2022).

Danticat, E. (2000). AHA! In M.N. Danquaah (ed.), *Becoming an American: Personal Essays by First Generation Immigrant Women* (pp. 39–44). New York: Hyperion.

Denborough, D. (2014). *Retelling the Stories of Our Lives: Everyday Narrative Therapy to Draw Inspiration and Transform Experience*. New York: W.W. Norton & Company.

Derrida, J. (1996). *Monolingualism of the Other and the Prosthesis of Origin*, trans. P. Mensah. Stanford, CA: Stanford University Press.

Dewing, M. (2013). *Canadian Multiculturalism: Background Paper* (Publication No.2009-20-E). Library of Parliament, 1–23.

Dockery, W. (2017). Germany and refugees: A chronology. dw.com, 4 September. https://www.dw.com/en/two-years-since-germany-opened-its-borders-to-refugees-a-chronology/a-40327634 (accessed 29 January 2023).

Douglas, J., Hulshof, K., Motus, N., Naciri, M., & Nishimoto, T. (2020). End stigma and discrimination against migrant workers and their children during COVID-19 pandemic. ReliefWeb, 9 June. https://reliefweb.int/report/world/end-stigma-and-discrimination-against-migrant-workers-and-their-children-during-covid (Accessed 29 May 2020).

Douglas Brown, H. (1980). *Principles of Language Learning and Teaching*. New Jersey: Prentice Hall.

REFERENCES

Eagleton, T. (1983). *Literary Theory: An Introduction.* Minneapolis, MN: University of Minnesota Press.

Eco, U. (2004). *On Literature,* trans. M. McLaughlin. Orlando, FL: Harcourt.

Enriquez de Salamanca, C. (2020). Rites of passage in migration and adolescence: struggling in transformation. In K. White & I. Klingenberg (eds), *Migration and Intercultural Psychoanalysis: Unconscious Forces and Clinical Issues* (pp. 108–19). London: Routledge.

Ensor, M. (2016). South Sudanese diaspora children: contested notions of childhood, uprootedness, and belonging among young refugees in the U.S. In M.L. Seeberg & E.M. Goździak (eds), *Contested Childhoods: Growing Up in Migrancy: Migration, Governance, Identities* (pp. 61–77). Springer Open.

European Parliament: Legislative Train Schedule, towards a New Policy on Migration (2016). EU–Turkey Statement and Action Plan. http://www.europarl.europa.eu/legislative-train/theme-towards-a-new-policy-on-migration/file-eu-turkey-statement-action-plan (Accessed 9 June 2018).

Felman, S. (1987). *Jacques Lacan and the Adventure of Insight Psychoanalysis in Contemporary Culture.* Cambridge, MA: Harvard University Press.

——— (2011). *The Future of Testimony.* Conference, University of Salford, Manchester, UK.

Felman, S., & Laub, D. (1992). *Testimony: Crises of Witnessing in Literature, Psychoanalysis, and History.* New York, NY: Routledge.

Fernando, J. (2018). Trauma and the zero process: clinical illustrations. *Psychoanalysis,* 29 (3), 37–45. https://doi.org/10.18529/psychoanal.2018.29.3.37

——— (2022, October 22). *Trauma, Guilt, and Conspiracy: The Zero Process and the Superego.* Scientific Program Meeting, Ottawa Psychoanalytic Society.

Fivush, R., & Nelson, K. (2020). The development of autobiographical memory, autobiographical narratives, and autobiographical consciousness. *Psychological Reports,* 123(1), 71–96.

Fowler, J.C., Allen, J.G., Oldham, J.M., & Frueh, B.C. (2013). Exposure to interpersonal trauma, attachment insecurity, and depression severity. *Journal of Affective Disorders,* 149(1–3), 313–18. https://doi.org/10.1016/j.jad.2013.01.045

Freed, L. (2000). Embracing the alien. In M.N. Danquaah (ed.), *Becoming an American: Personal Essays by First Generation Immigrant Women* (pp. 55–67). New York: Hyperion.

Freud, A. (1967 [1953]) About losing and being lost. In R. Ekins and R. Freeman (eds), *Anna Freud: Selected Writings* (pp. 97–108). New York: Penguin.

——— (1998a). Observations on child development. In R. Ekins and R. Freeman (eds), *Anna Freud: Selected Writings* (pp. 50–66). New York: Penguin.

REFERENCES

———— (1998b). Adolescence. In R. Ekins and R. Freeman (eds), *Anna Freud: Selected Writings* (pp: 181–205). New York: Penguin.

Freud, S. (1920–55). *The Standard Edition of the Complete Psychological Works of Sigmund Freud*, ed. A. Freud, A. Strachey, & A. Tyson, 24 vols (1953–74). London: Hogarth.

———— (1927). Some psychological consequences of the anatomical distinction between the sexes. *International Journal of Psychoanalysis*, 8, 133–42.

———— (1931). Female sexuality. In *The Standard Edition of the Complete Psychological Works of Sigmund Freud*, Vol. 21 (1927–31): *The Future of an Illusion, Civilization and its Discontents, and Other Works* (pp. 221–44).

———— (1930, 2002c). *Civilization and its Discontents*, trans. D. Mclintock. In A. Phillips (ed.), *The Freud Reader*. New York: Penguin.

———— (2006). Beyond the pleasure principle. In A. Phillips (ed.), *The Freud Reader*. (pp. 132–95). New York: Penguin.

Gallop, J. (2012). Lacan's 'mirror stage': where to begin. *Substance*, *1982/1983*, 11(4)–12(1), Issues 37–38, 118–28. https://doi.org/10.2307/3684185

Gilbert, J. (2010). Reading histories: curriculum theory, psychoanalysis, and generational violence. In E. Malewski (ed.), *Curriculum Studies Handbook: The Next Moment* (pp. 63–72). New York: Routledge.

Global Detention Project (2018). *Immigration Detentions in Canada: Important Reforms, Ongoing Concerns*. https://www.globaldetentionproject.org/countries/americas/canada (accessed 10 November 2019).

Goździak, E. (2016). Forced victims or willing migrants? In M.L. Seeberg & E.M. Goździak (eds), *Contested Childhoods: Growing Up in Migrancy: Migration, Governance, Identities* (pp. 23–41). Springer Open.

Guiora, A., Brannon, R., & Dull, C. (1972). Empathy and second language learning. *Language Learning*, 22, 111–30.

Gutiérrez-Peláez, M. (2015). Ferenczi's anticipation of the traumatic dimension of language: a meeting with Lacan. *Contemporary Psychoanalysis*, 51(1), 137–54.

Herman-Peck, S., & Harrington, B. (2018). The 'Flores Settlement' and alien families apprehended at the U.S. border: frequently asked questions. *Current Politics and Economics of the United States*, 20(1), 107–33. https://fas.org/sgp/crs/homesec/R45297.pdf *(Accessed 17 August 2020)*.

Herrera, J. (2021). Biden brings back family separation—this time in Mexico. POLITICO, 20 March. https://www.politico.com/news/magazine/2021/03/20/border-family-separation-mexico-biden-477309 (accessed 5 December 2021).

Hodes, M., Mendoza-Vasquez, M., Anagnostopoulos, D., Triantafyllou, Abdelhady, D., Weiss, K., Koposov, R., Cuhadaroglu, F., Hebebrand, J., & Skokauskas, N. (2018). Refugees in Europe: national overviews from key countries with a special

REFERENCES

focus on child and adolescent mental health. *European Child & Adolescent Psychiatry*, 27, 389–99.

Homeland Security (2022). President Biden to announce Uniting for Ukraine, a new streamlined process to welcome Ukrainians fleeing Russia's invasion of Ukraine. https://www.dhs.gov/news/2022/04/21/president-biden-announce-uniting-ukraine-new-streamlined-process-welcome-ukrainians (Accessed 29 June 2022).

Hoppennot, E. (2014). The writing of disaster. *Témoigner. Entre histoire et mémoire*, 118, 193.

Johnston, A. (2022). Jacques Lacan: Otherness, the Oedipus complex, and sexuation. *Stanford Encyclopedia of Philosophy*. https://plato.stanford.edu/entries/lacan/ (Accessed 10 February 2023).

Juneau, G., & Rubin, N. (2014). *A First Person Account of the Refugee Experience*. American Psychological Association. https://www.apa.org/international/pi/2014/12/global-violence (accessed 29 January 2021).

Jung, Ha-yun (2004). Personal and singular. *Harvard Review*, 26, 165–74.

Karpinski, E. (2012). *Borrowed Tongues: Life Writing, Migration and Translation*. Waterloo, ON: Wilfred Laurier University Press.

Katz, I. (2016). A network of camps on the way to Europe. *Forced Migration Review: Destination Europe*, 51, 17–19. https://www.fmreview.org/sites/fmr/files/FMRdownloads/en/destination-europe.pdf (Accessed 1 April 2021).

Kellman, S. (ed.) (2003). *Switching Languages: Translingual Writers Reflect on their Craft*. Lincoln: University of Nebraska Press.

Klein, M. (1975). *Envy and Gratitude and Other Works*. New York: Free Press.

Klein, M., & Riviere, J. (1964). Love, guilt and reparation. In *Love, Hate and Reparation*, ed. M. Klein & J. Riviere. New York: W.W. Norton & Company.

Kramsch, C. (2009). *The Multilingual Subject: What Foreign Language Learners Say about their Experience and Why It Matters*. Oxford: Oxford University Press.

Kristeva, J. (1986). *Revolution in poetic language*. The Kristeva Reader. Ed. Toril Moi. New York: Columbia University Press, pp. 89–136.

Kronick, R., Rousseau, C., & Cleveland, J. (2018). Refugee children's sandplay narratives in immigration detention in Canada. *European Child & Adolescent Psychiatry*, 27, 423–37.

Lai, A., & Maclean, R. (2011). Children on the move: the impact of involuntary and voluntary migration on the lives of children. *Global Studies of Childhood*, 1(2), 87–91. https://www.wwwords.co.uk/GSCH (Accessed 10 July 2018).

Linton, J., Griffin, M., & Shapiro, A. (2017). Detention of immigrant children. *American Academy of Pediatrics*, 139(4), 1–13.

Luckhurst, R. (2008). *The Trauma Question*. New York: Routledge.

REFERENCES

Major, B., & O'Brien, L.T. (2005). The social psychology of stigma. *Annual Review of Psychology*, 56(1), 393–421. https://doi.org/10.1146/annurev.psych.56.091103.070137

McGregor, L.S., Melvin, G.A., & Newman, L.K. (2015). Differential accounts of refugee and resettlement experiences in youth with high and low levels of posttraumatic stress disorder (PTSD) symptomatology: a mixed-methods investigation. *American Journal of Orthopsychiatry*, 85(4), 371–81.

Measham, T., Guzder, J., Rousseau, C., Pacione, L., Blais-McPherson, M., & Nadeau, L. (2014). Refugee children and their families: supporting psychological well-being and positive adaptation following migration. *Current Problems in Pediatric Health Care*, 44(7), 208–15.

Mishra Tarc, A. (2015). *Literacy of the Other: Renarrating Humanity*, ed. D. Britzman. Albany: State University of New York Press.

Morrison, A., Fredricks, K., & Agrawal, N. (2018). Separated and sick: an immigrant child's traumatic experience of illness and recovery. *Pediatrics*, 142(6), 1–3.

Munro, M.J. (2003). A primer on accent discrimination in the Canadian context. *TESL Canada Journal*, 20(2), 38–51. https://doi.org/10.18806/tesl.v20i2.947

Neufeld, A. (2021). Doug Ford asked to apologize over 'divisive' comments about immigrants. CTV News, 18 October. https://toronto.ctvnews.ca/doug-ford-asked-to-apologize-over-divisive-comments-about-immigrants-1.5627943 (accessed 22 April 2022).

Ortiz Cofer, J. (2015). *The Cruel Country*. Athens, GA: University of Georgia Press.

Pallister-Wilkins, P. (2018). Hotspots and the geographies of humanitarianism. *Environment and Planning D: Society and Space*, 38(6), 991–1008.

Palmer, H. (1997). Mosaic Versus Melting Pot? Immigration and Ethnicity in Canada and the United States. In D. Taras & B. Rasporich (eds), *A Passion for Identity: Introduction to Canadian Studies* (pp. 82–96). Nelson Thornes Limited.

Pavlenko, A. (2007). Autobiographic narratives as data in applied linguistics. *Applied Linguistics*, 28(2), 163–88.

Phillips, A. (1998). *The Beast in the Nursery*. New York: Pantheon Books.

Pitt, A. (2006). Mother Love's education. In G. Boldt & P. Salvio (eds), *Love's Return: Psychoanalytic Essays on Childhood, Teaching and Learning* (pp. 87–106). New York: Routledge.

——— (2013). Language on loan: meditations on the emotional world of language learning and teaching. In J. Plews and B. Schmench (eds), *Traditions and Transitions: Curricula for German Studies*. Waterloo, ON: Wilfred Laurier University Press.

Riley, P. (1991). What's your background? The culture and identity of the bilingual child. In C. Brumfit, J. Moon, & R. Tongue (eds), *Teaching English to Children: From Practice to Principle*. New Jersey: Pearson English Language Teaching.

REFERENCES

Rosenblum, M. (2015). Unaccompanied child migration to the United States: the tension between protection and prevention. *Transatlantic Council on Migration: A Project of the Migration Policy Institute*, 1–33.

Saint-Onge, K. (2013). *Bilingual Being: My Life as a Hyphen*. Montreal, Que: McGill-Queen's University Press.

Sanderson, S. (2019). Minor killed at Moira migrant camp on Lesbos. *Info Migrants*. https://www.infomigrants.net/en/post/19064/minor-killed-at-moira-migrant-camp-on-lesbos (Accessed 8 September 2020).

Schweikart, S. (2019). April 2018 Flores Settlement suit challenges unlawful administration of psychotropic medication to immigrant children. *AMA Journal of Ethics*, 21(1), E67–72. https://doi.org/10.1001/amajethics.2019.67

Shahani, A.N. (2019). *Here We Are: American Dreams, American Nightmares*. New York: Celadon Books.

Simic, C. (1999). Refugees. In A. Aciman (ed.), *Letters of Transit: Reflections on Exile, Identity, Language, and Loss* (pp. 119–135). New York: New Press.

Stengel, E. (1939). On learning a new language. *International Journal of Psychoanalysis*, 20, 471–79.

Sutterlüty, F., & Tisdall, E.K.M. (2019). Agency, autonomy and self-determination: questioning key concepts of childhood studies. *Global Studies of Childhood*, 9(3), 183–87.

Taub, A. (2022). The Ukrainian refugee crisis is a women's crisis. *New York Times*, 13 April. https://www.nytimes.com/2022/04/13/world/europe/ukraine-refugees-women.html (accessed 22 April 2022).

Tazzioli, M. (2017). Containment through mobility: migrants' spatial disobediences and the reshaping of control through the hotspot system in the Mediterranean. *Journal of Ethnic and Migration Studies*, 44(16), 2764–79.

Thompson, Clara (1943). Penis envy in women. Psychiatry, 6(2), 123–25.

Tsekouras, P. (2022). Ontario earmarks $300 million in supports for Ukrainian refugees. CTV News, 6 April. https://toronto.ctvnews.ca/ontario-earmarks-300-million-in-supports-for-ukrainian-refugees-1.5850318 (accessed 22 April 2022).

Tuters, K. (2016). Childhood displacement and its impact on the formation of personality. *Japan Association of Infant Mental Health*, April, Tokyo.

Uwiringiyimana, S. (2017). *How Dare the Sun Rise: Memoirs of a War Child*. New York: HarperCollins.

van der Kolk, B., & van der Hart, O. (1995). The intrusive past: the flexibility of memory and the engraving of trauma. In C. Caruth (ed.), *Trauma: Explorations in Memory* (pp. 158–82). Baltimore: Johns Hopkins University Press.

REFERENCES

van Loenen, T., van den Muijsenbergh, M., Hofmeester, M., Dowrick, C., van Ginneken, N., Aggelos Mechili, E., Angelaki, A., Ajdukovic, D., Bakic, H., Rotar Pavlic, D., Zelko, E., Hoffman, K., Jirovsky, E., Mayrhuber, E.S., Dückers, M., Mooren, T., Gouweloos-Trines, J., Kolozsvári, L., Rurik, I., & Lionis, C. (2017). Primary care for refugees and newly arrived migrants in Europe: a qualitative study on health needs, barriers, and wishes. *European Journal of Public Health*, 28(1), 82–87.

Volkan, V.D. (2017). *Immigrants and Refugees: Trauma, Perennial Mourning, Prejudice, and Border Psychology*. London: Routledge.

Wamariya, C. (2018). *The Girl Who Smiled Beads: A Story of War and What Comes After*. Toronto: Penguin Random House.

Winnicott, D.W. (1986). *Home Is Where We Start From: Essays by a Psychoanalyst*. New York: W.W. Norton & Company.

——— (2005). *Playing and Reality*. New York: Routledge.

Yousafzai, M. (2019). *We Are Displaced: My Journey and Stories from Refugee Girls around the World*. Baltimore, MD: Johns Hopkins University Press.

Index

The letter 'n' indicates an endnote.

Abdelmahmoud, Elamin 120–1
'About losing and being lost'
(Anna Freud) 108–9, 110
accompanied children 38, 56, 125
see also unaccompanied children
acculturation 123, 127, 147n1
acquisition of knowledge 64
adaptive solutions 77–8
Al-Adeimi, M. 125, 126–7
adolescence: hating parents 75, 145n1;
individuation 104; physical and
emotional changes 59; psychoanalytic
literature 74–8; self-image 103;
significance of parental figures
71–4; socioemotional and sexual
development 78; subjective
experiences 42
adolescent migrants: conflicts from
changes 64, 102–3; and host
countries 89; international protection
24; risk of harassment and abuse 3;
separation-individuation phases 56;
travelling unaccompanied 2–4
Adorno, Theodor 46
adults: acculturation 127; ego
boundaries 103; post-migration
experiences 84–5
affective memory 83
Agamben, Giorgio 14, 15, 46
age 99, 145n7
'Aggression and the telos of language
learning' (Carra-Salsberg) 62, 64
Agosín, Marjorie 100

Agrawal, N. 39
Ajana, Btijhag 30
Akhtar, Salman: adults linguistic
changes 99; displacement 146n4;
human, universal needs 43, 87;
individuation 104; learning a
new language 62–3; mentation
48; newcomers grieving missed
experiences 102; primary languages
53; psychoanalytic approaches
84–5, 86; separation-individuation
phases 55–6
'aliens' (illegal migrants) 143n19
Amnesty International 20, 36–7
Ang, S. 19, 22
anger 78–9
anomia language tensions (Agamben)
46
anomie (Block) 100
anomie (Durkheim) 61–2, 63
anti-Chinese rhetoric 22
anti-human-trafficking training 125
anti-refugee and migrant discourses 120
Arendt, Hannah 9–10, 12, 121–2; *The
Human Condition* 10; interview with
Günter Gaus 13–15, 45–7; language
as a remnant 45–7; mortality 9;
mother tongue 47; natality 9, 64;
remembered history of oppression 47
art 73–4
asylum seekers 16–17, 32–3
Auschwitz 46
austerity migrants 27

INDEX

Australia 27
auto-narratives 7, 85, 87, 93, 110, 114–16 *see also* cross-cultural auto-narratives; first-person narratives
autobiographical memory 83–4

Baehr, P.R. 14, 45, 46
Bakhtin, Bakhtin 11
Bakhtin, Mikhail 12, 95, 139n4
Banyamulenge people (Congo) 15–16
Baranczak, S. 98–9
BBC News 20, 37
The Beast in the Nursery (Phillips) 53–4
Becoming American (Danticat) 26
Begley, Louis 110
belief systems 11, 102
Bemak, F.D. 119, 120, 123, 124, 126
Berry, John W. 147n1
'Beyond the pleasure principle' (Sigmund Freud) 70, 115
Biden administration 20, 21, 36–7
Bilingual Being (Saint-Onge) 56
bilingualism 100
bisexual fluidity 94
Blanchot, Maurice 69–71
Block, David 59, 60, 61, 63, 99, 100
Bohórquez-Arcila, Paola 146n2
boys: ego development and Oedipal Complex 94; mother as first love object 146n1
Brannon, R. 58
Britzman, Deborah 48, 54–5, 62, 146–7n6
Brown, J. 125, 126–7
Burgos, M. 125, 126–7
Butler, Judith 14, 15

Camus, Albert 91–2
Canada 19; children and family units 33; culture 23; detaining children 40, 41–2; detaining illegal entrants 27; detention holding centres 41, 144n22; 'foreign nationals' (illegal migrants) 143n19; geographic restrictionism 23; historical responses to transnational movements 22–3; Immigration and Refugee Protection Act (IRPA) 40–1, 143n20; immigration detentions 40–2, 143n17; minors 41–2; Multicultural Policy 40; point-based approach to immigration 23; racialization and bias 21; unlawful entries 40–1; World War II attitudes towards migrants 23
Canada Border Services Agency (CBSA) 41
canonization 11, 139n3
carceral environments: children 27, 37–8, 40, 41–2; segregated by gender 41; violence 31; vulnerable individuals 40 *see also* detention centres
caregivers' absences 114
Cariola, Laura 54
Carra-Salsberg, Fernanda 62, 64
Caruth, Cathy 44, 82, 84, 95
Central Nervous System (CNS) 84
child–adult separations 2–3; children feeling abandoned 42; and human trafficking 36–7; politically motivated 35; processing centres 34–6
child–mother bond 55
child–mother boundaries 49
child–parent estrangement 111–14
childhood trauma 97
children 36; adults' influence 105–7; affected by stigmatizing 145n9; capacity for love 72–3; changes in reality and identity 102–3; detaining 27, 33–4, 37–8, 40, 41–2; development within language, otherness, and trauma 48–51; emotional growth and primary caregivers 71, 73; first self-love 49; human trafficking and exploitation 33; immigration processes 38; incestual desire 50; international protection 24; introjecting societal rules 50; *lalangue* 49; matricide 64, 111; migration 78–80; phantastical aggression 72; post-migration experiences 84–5; pre-Oedipal period 49; psycho-emotional and social development 54; psychosexual development 48–9, 71; psychosexual relationships 94; risk of harassment and abuse 3; self-image 103; selfhood 49–50; separation-individuation phases 55–6; significance of parental figures 71–4; socioemotional and sexual development 78; subjective experiences 42; travelling alone 36;

INDEX

unsuccessful asylum seekers 29; US processing and customs enforcement residential centres 37–9; weak language ego 59; young migrants 2–3 *see also* minors; mothers

Chung, R.C.-Y. 119, 120, 123, 124, 126

civilian guilt 14

Civilization and its Discontents (Sigmund Freud) 47

Cleveland, Janet 42

'climate refugees' 139n1

cognitive adaptation 65

Collett, Elizabeth 141–2n5

coming-to-consciousness 11, 139n4

compassion 43

conceptualizing the conscious and unconscious guilt 86

Congo (DRC) 15–16

Covid-19 20, 22

creativity 73–4

crime rates 120

criminalizing illegal migration 27

cross-cultural auto-narratives 90, 92–3, 97, 106, 121 *see also* auto-narratives; translingual auto-narratives

cross-cultural publications 85–6

The Cruel Country (Ortiz Cofer) 105–7

cultural identity 102

culturally informed interventions 124

culturally responsive care 125

culture shocks 106

Danticat, Edwidge 26–7

day-to-day interactions 11

deculturation 147n1

deeds defining us 10

defence against object love 76

defence of 'turning against the self' (Anna Freud) 79

'defense by displacement of libido' (Anna Freud) 76

'defense by regression' (Anna Freud) 76–7

'defense by reversal of affect' (Anna Freud) 76

'defense by withdrawal of libido to the self' (Anna Freud) 76

Democratic Republic of the Congo (DRC) 15–16

Denborough, David 96, 115

deporting asylum seekers 35, 36, 143n12 *see also* Title 42 (USA)

depression 106

Derrida, J. 11–12

destination countries' receiving systems 18

detainees mental healthcare 143n18

detaining children 33–4, 40, 41–2

detaining illegal entrants 27

detention centres 31, 33–4, 39–40, 144n22 *see also* carceral environments

development of an organized personality theory (Winnicott) 59

developmental and authoritative meaning of language theory (Lacan) 93

developmental theory (Winnicott) 114

The Dialogic Imagination (Bakhtin) 11

differentiable memory systems 83–4

disconnection with parents 112

discrimination 119–20; acculturation and adjustment 127; adults idealization of heritage 126; harassment and abuse 3; immigration policies and receiving systems 27; and marginalization 123

disillusionment: and resentment of role reversals 105; and weaning 52; world of adults 55–6

disorienting conscious 101

displacement 58, 103, 146n4 *see also* marginalization

displacement of affect theory (Anna Freud) 110

distancing from former life 103

dominant groups 22, 145n9

dominant ideological beliefs 17–19

Douglas, J. 3

Douglas Brown, H. (1980) 58–9

Dull, C. 58

Durkheim, Émile 61, 63

Eagleton, T. 50

Eastern Europe 20

Eco, Umberto 11

economic migrants 2

education 3–4 *see also* schools

ego: adolescents 76–7; battles with the id 76; interpretation of learning 67–8; learner's inner and outer realities 62

ego boundaries 58, 76, 99

INDEX

ego development 58–9, 94, 99
ego identification 49
ego permeability 99
ego psychology 79
emotional discontinuity 113
emotional insecurity 78–9
emotional memory 83
emotional safety 43
Encyclopedia of Personality and Individual Differences (Cariola) 54
English language 107–10
Enriquez de Salamanca, Celia 78–9, 80
episodic memory 83
ethos of violence 15–17
Etobicoke, Canada 21
EU receiving states 28–9
EU–Turkey Joint Action Plan (2016) 141n5
Europe: border management system 28–9; critical border zones 30; dispersing and mobilizing migrants 31; migrants' specific pathways 141n2; unauthorized arrivals 27; unsuccessful asylum seekers 29
experiential realities 87
explicit memory 83
extreme poverty 24

families 2–3, 27, 32–9, 128–9
family cohesion 126
family residential centres 38
family units 33–4, 35, 36–7
Felman, Shoshana 46, 50, 92
Fernando, Joseph 83–4, 86, 97
financial costs of migrants 18–19
finding meaning within 11–12
first-generation migrants 57, 58
first individuation 53, 120
first languages 100, 109 *see also* mother tongue
first-person narratives 92, 114, 121 *see also* auto-narratives
first-person singular narratives 108
Fivush, R. 147n2
flight risks 27, 41, 142n9, 144n21
Flores Settlement Agreement 33–4, 39, 140n12
forced relocations 17
Ford, Doug 21
foreign-host linguistic code 100
foreign information 62

foreign-language immersion 99
foreign–other dichotomy 65–6
foster care 34, 38, 41, 118, 140n11
    see also unaccompanied children
Foucault, Michel 145n8
foundational years 112, 113
Frames of War (Butler) 14
Fredricks, K. 39
Freed, L. 117
freedom through action 9
Freud, Anna: adolescence and infancy 74–8; displacement of affect theory 110; losing object of emotional importance 110; material possessions and love objects 108–9; 'Observations on child development' 71–2; reflexive process of projection 79
Freud, Sigmund: *Civilization and Its Discontents* 46–7; fixation with distressing events 70; girls' development 146n1; Oedipal Complex 49, 71, 94, 144n1, 144n3
The Future of Testimony (Felman) 46

Gatumba Massacre 98
Gaus, Günter 13, 45, 46, 48
genocide 14, 17
geographic restrictionism 23
Germany 13–14, 19, 140n10
Gilbert, Jennifer 63–4
The Girl Who Smiled Beads (Wamariya) 96–7, 111–13
girls' development 146n1
global challenges 18
Global Detention Project (GDP) 33, 40, 41, 143n14, 143n15
'good enough mothers' 52
Goździak, E.M. 140n13
Greece 28–9, 140n9, 141n1, 141n5
Green, André 64
grief 105–6
Griffin, M. 35, 36, 142n7
group membership 60
Guiora, A. 58
Gutiérrez-Peláez, M. 49, 51

Haiti 26
Hart, O. van der 82–3, 86–7, 145n2, 145n6
healthcare 31, 124
healthy and stable attachments 79–80

151

INDEX

healthy child–parent relationships 72, 79

hegemonic relations 21, 27, 60, 66, 145n8

Herrera, J. 32

Ho, E. 19, 22

Hodes, M. 140n9

Holocaust 9, 14, 145n9

home countries 32

Home Is Where We Start From (Winnicott) 73

homelessness 112

homes as places of safety 47

homesickness 105

Hoppenot, Éric 70

host countries: benefits of inclusion and diversity 129; connection and belongingness 89; United States 140n9

host-cultural adjustment 101

host cultures 85

host language: dominance 107; subjectivity when translating 101; writing, and transformation 107–11 *see also* second language

host-language acquisition: appearing comic 59–60, 67; initial stages of linguistic and cultural immersion 58; internalization 63; parents' social and navigational capital 127; strain between children and caregivers 65 *see also* language acquisition

hotspots 28, 30–1, 141n1

How Dare the Sun Rise (Uwiringiyimana) 15, 60, 101–2

The Human Condition (Arendt) 10

human connectedness 71

human suffering 123

human trafficking: educating and assessing scope of 125; impact on separations 36–7; indirect involvement 125, 147n3; reporting suspicions 125; unaccompanied children 33, 34–5

humanitarian corridors 27

humanitarian crises 122

humanness 9–10

id and ego battles 77

idealizing heritage language, traditions and culture 57, 101, 126

ideational and relational dissonance 104

identifications 55

ideological webs 19

illegal foreigners 30

illegal migrants 27

imaginary register 49–51

immersion in new languages 67

immigrants' recollections *see* memories

immigration: discrimination in policies 27; open-door policies 19, 123–5, 140n10; quotas 22–3; racism, and racialization 19–22

impersonal traumas 118

implicit memory 83

Individual Education Plans (IEP) 128

individuation 55–6, 104, 120

infantile history of object relations 78–9

infants: 'good enough mother' 52; pre-existing realities and frameworks 12; subjectivity 49 *see also* Oedipal Complex (Sigmund Freud)

'insider versus outsider' instincts 65

integration/bicultural period of acculturation 147n1

internalization of negative stereotypes 120–1

internalization of populist views 120

internalized language 4–5, 12, 63, 66

internalized linguistic code 99, 119

internalized white supremacy 121

international migrations 118

international protection 24

international relocations 1–2, 85, 87–9, 115, 122

international students 2

interpersonal traumas 81, 86, 118

intra-subjective splits 106

irregular migrants 28, 30–1

Italy 28–9, 141n1

Janet, Pierre 84, 145n2, 147n2

Japan 27

Johnston, Adrian 94

Jones, Ernest 75

jouissance (enjoyment) 49, 144n4

Jung, Ha-yun 107–9

justice systems 124

Karpinski, Eva 101

Kellman, Stephen 99

Klein, Melanie 72–3, 74, 75, 79, 145n1

152

INDEX

Kleinian theory 145n9
Kolk, B. van der 82–3, 86–7, 145n2, 145n6
Korean 108, 109–10
Kramsch, Claire 10–11
Kristeva, Julia 94, 95
Kronick, Rachel 42

Lacan, Jacques 47, 48–9, 50, 93, 94–5, 144n1, 144n2
lalangue 47, 49, 51, 94–5
Lambert, [name required] 60, 61, 63, 100
language: ability to heal 115; and affect 93; anomia and the norm 46; belonging/unbelonging 119; conscious and unconscious interactions 48; earliest experiences 108; gender, and psychoanalysis 93–5; and group membership 60; and identification 54–5; and individuations 55–7; influential nature 12–13; known and unknown dynamics 48; and *lalangue* 51, 94; links to the external world 44–5; psycho-emotional and social meanings 45; as a remnant 45–7; semiotic lens 11, 119; and the Shoah 13; and subjectivity 10–13; and transference 79–80; writing and transformation 107–10
language acquisition: anachronic act 61; anxiety, discomfort and age 145n7; emotional responses 60–2; migrants' translating realities 58–60; traumas 62–3 *see also* host-language acquisition; second language
language ego 59
language fluency 145n8
'Language on loan' (Pitt) 61
language socialization 115
learning to be human 10
legal migrants 24
Lesbos, Greece 142n6
Levi, Primo 14, 15
libidinal development 71–2
libido directions 77–8
libido displacement 75–6
Linda, Pastor 103–4
linguistic lacerations 110
Linton, J. 35, 36, 142n7

lived languages 12
living creatively 73–4
Loenen, T. van 31
'Love, guilt and reparation' (Klein) 75
Luckhurst, Roger 81

Major, B. 65
makeshift encampments 29, 32
marginalization 16, 26–7, 58, 66 *see also* displacement
matricide 64, 111
McGregor, L.S. 88–9
Measham, T. 122, 124
media 1, 122, 142n6
Melvin, G.A. 88–9
memories: of displacement 92; distorted 145n2; early events and of stressful events 147n2; immigrants' recollections 85; of love and first language 109; and trauma 82–4, 85
mental health 124, 143n18
mentation 48, 83
mentorship programmes 125
Mexico 27, 32–3, 140n9
migrant camps 30
migrants 2–4; children's individuation 56; crime rates 120; financial costs 18–19; medical and healthcare challenges 31; sense of loss and grief 105
migrations 1; child–parent estrangements 111–14; international migrations 118; legal and planned 118; and trauma 80–1
Miłosz, Czesław 99
'Minor killed at Moira migrant camp on Lesbos' (Sanderson) 142n6
minors 2–3; acculturation 129; awareness of their parents' struggles 127; ego boundaries 99; human trafficking 34–5; individuations 120; overcrowded holding facilities 35; positive adaptations 125; post-migration struggles 123; stereotyping and amplifying awareness 128–9 *see also* children; mothers
mirror stage 49–50
Mishra Tarc, Aparna 12
monolingual migrants 58, 85, 99
Monolingualism of the Other (Derrida) 12
moral responsiveness 14

153

INDEX

Morrison, A. 39
mortality (Arendt) 9
mother–father binary 94
mother tongue 53–4; resistance to switching languages 99; speaker's history of affect 107; switching internal languages 100; universal guilt from replacing 57 *see also* primary language
mothers: child's first self-love 49; child's socio-emotional development 71–2 *see also* children; minors
The Multilingual Subject (Kramsch) 10–11
'multilingualism' (Bakhtin) 11
myelinization 58, 67, 145n6

narrative memory 83–4
narrative therapy 96
natality (Arendt) 2, 64
need for normalcy 13–14
need for self-preservation 14
need for silence 14
need to forget 14
need to recall and share 85–6
need to testify/bear witness 86
Nelson, K. 147n2
never-ending present 101
New York 91–2
newcomers: acculturation and political climates 123; disorienting effects 85; experiences as point of reference 102; financial struggles 3; foreign-language immersion 99; grieving missed experiences 102; imaginable and unimaginable experiences 17–18; immersion in new languages 67; introjection of new languages 62–3; loss and mourning their past 85; loss in experiential continuity 101; low wages and underemployment 127; mental health and well-being 124; preconscious experiences of trauma 84–6; socio-psychological challenges 115; testimonial experiences 87
Newman, L.K. 88–9
non-secure state-licensed facilities 33–4
the norm language tensions (Agamben) 46
nostalgia 111
Novel Education (Britzman) 48

O'Brien, L.T. 65
'oceanic feelings' (Arendt) 47
Oedipal Complex (Sigmund Freud) 49, 71, 94, 144n1, 144n3 *see also* infants
Oedipal triangulation 144n2
omnipotence and compliance 73
'On being an orphaned writer' (Begley) 110
Ontario, Canada 21
open-door policies 19, 123–5, 140n10
oppressive conceptualizations 15
Oprah show 111
ordinary memory 83–4
original linguistic-cultural groups 63
Ortiz Cofer, Judith 105–7
the Other in translingual auto-narratives 93–5

parent–child communication 126–7
parent–child confrontations 57
parental absence 112
parents: acculturation 127; children's and adolescents' development 78; displacement 103–5; maintaining past cultural beliefs 57 *see also* primary caregivers
Pavlenko, Aneta 96, 114
'Pedagogy and clinical knowledge' (Britzman and Pitt) 62
'penis envy' (Freud) 146n1
'Personal and singular' (Jung) 107–8
personality and healthy development theory (Winnicott) 51–2
phallic signifiers 146n1
phantastical violence 64, 72
Phillips, Adam 53–4
physical safety 3, 33, 43
Piaget, Jean 54, 82–3
Pitt, Alice 54, 61, 62, 64
places of containment 30 *see also* hotspots
Playing and Reality (Winnicott) 51–2, 113
point-based approach to immigration 23, 24
popularist modern-day politics 120
The Portable Hannah Arendt 13
positive interactions and connections 89
post 9/11 attitudes 14
post-secondary programmes 129
post-structural anxiety 50

INDEX

post-structural view on language and power (Foucault) 145n8
post-traumatic growth 123
Post-Traumatic Stress Disorder (PTSD) 2, 30, 82, 88–9
pre-crossing separations 35
pre-Oedipal period 49
pre-war Germany 45–6
preconscious traumas 85, 86, 118
prejudicial attitudes 119–20
'Primary care for refugees and newly arrived migrants in Europe' (van Loenen) 31
primary caregivers 54, 71, 73, 126 *see also* parents
primary language 51–4, 55, 60–1, 100–1 *see also* mother tongue
primary symbolic code 68, 95, 100 *see also* symbolic code of meanings
procedural memory 83
processing centres 33–4, 38
projective identification 145n9
psychoanalysis: internalized linguistic code 119; post-migration experiences 84–5; primary caregivers and children's psychosexual and emotional growth 71; significance of parental figures 71–4
psychoanalytic theories 67, 89–90
psychoanalytic vantage points 94, 115
puberty 55–6, 74
published self-narratives 96
published testimonials 121
Puerto Rico 105
push factors 8, 25, 36, 87, 117

qualitative data 121

racialization 19–22, 25, 27, 127
racism 19–22, 27, 119–20, 127
Reading Histories (Gilbert) 63–4
'the Real' realm 50–1
receiving centres 31
receiving countries: challenges 18; detention and processing centres 33; Germany as model 140n10; open-door policies 124–5; post-secondary programmes 129; stigma 119; unwelcoming 29
recollection of traumatic events *see* memories

reconstruct (Blanchot) 70
reconstructed experiences 98, 114 *see also* auto-narratives; first-person narratives
reconstructing experiences 98
recurrent marginalization 26–7 *see also* marginalization
'Refugee children's sandplay narratives in immigration detention in Canada' (Kronick, Rousseau, & Cleveland) 42
Refugee Convention 1951 17
refugees: definition 17; evidence of persecution 24; shifting perspectives 21
rejecting parents' values 104
relational displacement 103, 146n4
relocation challenges 124
Remnants of Auschwitz (Agamben) 46
resettlement countries 17–18, 127
residential centres 143n13
Retelling the Stories of Our Lives (Denborough) 96
return to normalcy 14
returning to home country 32
Revolution of Poetic Language (Kristeva) 94
Riley, Philip 60
Riviere, Joan 72, 74, 75
role reversals 105
Rousseau, Cécile 42
Russia 21
Rwanda 15–16
Rwanda Massacre 96–7

Saint-Onge, Kathleen 56
Sanderson, S. 142n6
Sandler, Anne-Marie 103
Sandler, Joseph 103
sayable and unsayable in speech 46
Schacter, Daniel L. 83
schools 124, 127–8 *see also* education
second individuation 120
second language: accents as markers 60; children second method of play 59; distancing from first loves 61; emotionality 60–2; medium of self-expression 109; refusal to use 99 *see also* host language; language acquisition
Second Language Identities (Block) 59, 63

INDEX

second-language learners' experiences 60
second separation-individuation 55
secondary identifications 54–5
self-image 103
self-narratives 87
selfhood 49–50
semantic memory 83–4
semiotic lens 11
semiotic repression 94
semiotic-symbolic modalities 94–5
'Separated and sick' (Morrison, Fredricks and Agrawal) 39
separation-individuation phases 55–6 *see also* child–adult separations
Shahani, Aarti 56–7
Shapiro, A. 35, 36, 142n7
shared trauma 98
shelters 20, 33, 37, 140n11, 142n7, 143n13
significant learning 63–4
Simic, Charles 18
Singapore 22
smuggling minors 32
social uncertainty 61–2
socio-emotional affiliations 63
socio-psychological challenges 115
'soft' violence 17
'Some problems of adolescence' (Jones) 75
Son of Elsewhere (Abdelmahmoud) 121
South Kivu, DRC 15
speech 10
speech production 59–60
Stengel, E. 59, 61, 145n7
stigmatization 3, 65–6, 119
Strange Lands conference (2012) 84–5, 99, 146n3
'stranger danger' 66
stressors 88
substandard housing 3
superego 50, 55, 59–60, 74, 76, 104
supportive homes 78 *see also* families
Sutterlüty, F. 2
switching languages 99–101
Switching Languages (Kellman) 99
symbolic code of meanings 12, 13–15, 44–5, 58, 119, 146n2, 146n6 *see also* primary symbolic code
Symbolic Order 49–51, 67, 94, 118
symbolic registers 12, 50–1

Syrian crisis (2015) 19, 140n10, 141–2n5

Tazzioli, M. 28, 30, 31, 141n3, 141n4
temporal reality and continuity 87
temporary workers 2
thinking and humanness 9–10
third individuation 120
third-person plural narratives 108
third space 146–7n6
Thompson, Clara 146n1
Three Essays on the Theory of Sexuality (Sigmund Freud) 74
Tijuana, Mexico 32–3, 35
Tisdall, E.K.M. 2
Title 42 (USA) 20, 35, 37 *see also* deporting asylum seekers
transcultural auto-narratives 121 *see also* cross-cultural auto-narratives
transference 79–80
transit and receiving countries 28–9, 32–4, 119, 123, 140n9
transitional objects 52–3, 113
transitional phenomenon theory (Winnicott) 113
translingual auto-narratives 93–5, 114
translingual reconstructions 86
translingual subject 146n2
translingual writers 99
'translingualism' 146n2
transnational movements 1, 22–4
Trauma (Caruth) 95
trauma-informed care 124
traumas 2; being on the move 30–1; impersonal, interpersonal and preconscious 81–2, 118; international migrants' auto-narratives 87; intra-subjective splits 86–8; language and the remaking of the self 96–8; and memory 82–4; migrant camps 30; projective identification 145n9; transference 81, 145n9
traumatic dimensions of language 51
traumatic histories 69–70
traumatic memories 82–4, 85
tribal behaviour 65
Trump administration 20, 35, 36–7
Turkey 140n9, 141–2n5
'turning against the self' defence (Anna Freud) 79

INDEX

Ukrainian crisis 20–1, 27
unaccompanied children 20; culturally
  responsive care 125; deportations
  35; detaining 33–4, 37; and families
  relocating 118; human trafficking 33,
  34–5; illegal crossings and families
  27; mentorship programmes 125; US
  processing and customs enforcement
  residential centres 37–9 *see also*
  accompanied children; foster care
unauthorized migrants on the move 31
the unconscious 95
unconscious crises 101
unconscious 'give and take' 48, 146n6
unconscious responses 66
unconscious shift 146n4
understanding through self-expression
  107–8
undocumented children 3–4, 35
undocumented workers 3
unintegrated personalities 114
United Kingdom 27
United Nations Convention of the
  Rights of the Child (UNCRC) 24
United Nations High Commissioner for
  Refugees (UNHCR) 139n1
United States 27, 105; asylum
  seekers in Tijuana 32–3; attitudes
  to immigration 36–7; Biden
  administration 20, 21, 36–7;
  border policies 19–20; conditions
  for unaccompanied minors and
  families 39; Department of Health
  and Human Services (DHH)
  143n13; Department of Homeland
  Security 37; detention centres
  39–40; Flores Settlement Agreement
  33–4, 39, 140n12; host country
  140n9; Mexico border 20, 32–3;
  Office of Refugee Resettlement
  (ORR) 143n13; post 9/11 attitudes
  14; processing and customs
  enforcement residential centres 37–9;
  separations politically motivated 35;
  shelters 20, 33, 37, 140n11, 142n7,
  143n13; 'soft' violence 17; subtle
  violence 17; Title 42 20, 35, 37;
  trafficked children 33, 36; Trump
  administration 20, 35, 36–7; zero-
  tolerance policies 142n10

universal needs 43, 87
universal trauma 51
unprotected minors 3
unsuccessful asylum seekers 29
Uvira, South Kivu, DRC 16, 102,
  139n5
Uwiringiyimana, Sandra 15–17, 60,
  97–8, 101–2, 103–4

van der Hart, O. 82–3, 86–7, 145n2,
  145n6
van der Kolk, B. 82–3, 86–7, 145n2,
  145n6
van Loenen, T. 31
victim-centred programmes 125
victims of distressing events 70
violence 31, 142n6
Volkan, V.D. 65–6, 145n9
vulnerable individuals 40, 143n16

Wamariya, Clementine 96–7, 111–13,
  114, 116
weaning 52, 144n5
'What's your background?' (Riley) 60
Winnicott, D.W. 108; cultural space
  48; developmental theory 51–2, 59,
  114; *Home Is Where We Start From*
  73; individuation 55–6; *Playing and
  Reality* 51–2, 113; transitional objects
  52–3, 113; transitional phenomenon
  theory 113; weaning 144n5
Women in the World Summit 98
'Words: a basket of love' (Agosín) 100
World War II 13–14, 69–70
writers' pre-migration traumas 115
writing 95–6
Writing of the Disaster (Blanchot) 70
written testimonies 114

xenophobia 120, 127 *see also* racism

Yeoh, B. 19, 22
young migrants: experiences within
  languages 44–5; foreign-host
  sociolinguistic transformations
  101–5; stress of border crossings 2–3;
  support systems 127
Yousafzai, M. 1

zero-tolerance policies 35, 142n10